TRADITIONAL NEEDLE ARTS

CROSS STITCH

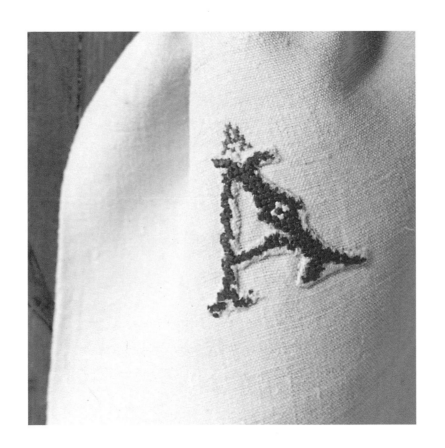

TRADITIONAL NEEDLE ARTS

CROSS STITCH

More than 30 classic projects

KATRIN CARGILL

PHOTOGRAPHY BY

DAVID MONTGOMERY

THUNDER BAY
P·R·E·S·S

To my nieces, Katrina and Lottie, with love

Published by
Thunder Bay Press
5880 Oberlin Drive, Suite 400
San Diego, California 92121

First published in Great Britain in 1994 by
Mitchell Beazley
an imprint of Reed Consumer Books Limited
Michelin House, 81 Fulham Road, London SW3 6RB
and Auckland, Melbourne, Singapore and Toronto

Art Director   JACQUI SMALL
Executive Editor   JUDITH MORE
Executive Art Editor   LARRAINE SHAMWANA
Editor   MARGOT RICHARDSON
Production   ALISON MYER
Design   MAGGIE TOWN & BOBBY BIRCHALL
Photographer   DAVID MONTGOMERY
Charts   RAYMOND & HELENA TURVEY
Illustrations   JANE HUGHES

Library of Congress Cataloging-in-Publication data

Cargill, Katrin.
Cross stitch: more than 30 nostalgic step-by-step projects/
Katrin Cargill; photography by David Montgomery.
p. cm. - (Traditional needle arts)
Includes index.
ISBN 1-57145-011-4 : $15.95
1. Cross-stitch - Patterns. 2. Household linens.
I. Title. II. Series.
TT778.C76C37 1994   94-16515
746.44'3041 - dc20   CIP

The publishers have made every effort to ensure that all
instructions given in this book are accurate and safe but they
cannot accept liability for any resulting injury, damage or loss
to either person or property, whether direct or consequential
and howsoever arising.
The author and publishers will be grateful for any
information which will assist them in keeping future editions
up to date.

Typeset in Perpetua 12/16pt and 10/12pt
Index compiled by Ingrid Lock
Printed and bound in Great Britain
by Butler & Tanner Ltd.

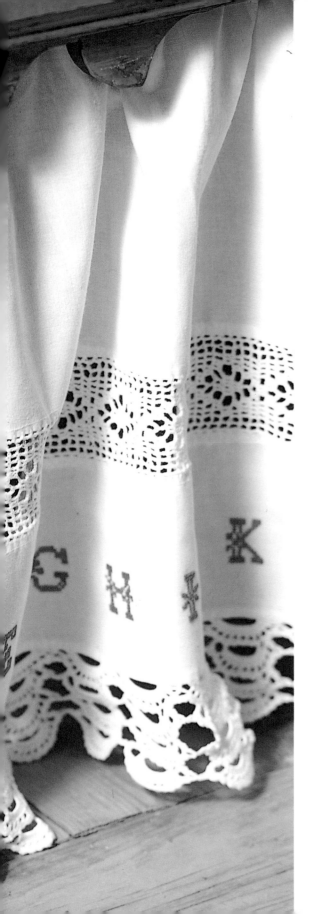

Contents

INTRODUCTION	7
BEFORE YOU BEGIN	12
SAMPLERS	17
Alphabet Sampler	18
Grace Shaw Sampler	25
House Sampler	30
TABLE LINEN	39
Napkins and Napkin Rings	41
Table Mats	44
Rose Tablecloth	50
Carnation Tablecloth	55
Peacock Tablecloth	59
Fringed Tablecloth	62
Tasseled Cloth	67
Reindeer Runner	70
BED LINEN	75
Sheet and Pillowcase	76
Feather Bedspread	83
Cradle Cover	86
ACCESSORIES	93
Carnation Pillow Cover	95
Rustic Pillow Cover	98
Tiebacks	102
Drapes	107
Figured Hand Towel	110
Book Covers	115
Lavender Sachets	118
Pincushion Boxes	123
INDEX	126
ACKNOWLEDGMENTS	128

Introduction

TOP Letters embroidered on a loose-weave linen the easiest type of fabric on which to learn cross stitch.
RIGHT AND BELOW LEFT Finely woven cotton with tiny stitches requires experience, but the delicate patterns are worth the work.
BELOW RIGHT A typical Aida fabric, where one stitch takes in two threads, both vertically and horizontally.
OPPOSITE LEFT A delicately embroidered hand towel from Russia.
RIGHT The simple art of cross stitch.

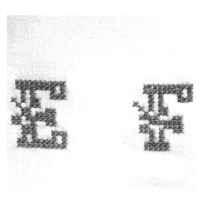

The history of cross stitch is almost as old as that of the human race. Cross stitch is the most ancient and basic form of stitching, used by early people in a crude form to lace animal skins together for clothing and shelter. Yet, from these rough, ready, and entirely practical beginnings, cross stitch has developed into a highly decorative and colorful craft. It has been used for centuries throughout the ancient world for embellishing clothing and household items, as it is both simple to execute and visually very pleasing.

Almost every culture has employed some kind of cross stitch. Pieces of decorative work have been found in countries as diverse as China, Uzbekistan, Morocco, Thailand, Mexico, Russia, South America, and all over Europe. Not surprisingly, each country seems to have developed its own distinctive style of color and pattern, and use for cross-stitched fabrics.

In China, for example, cross stitch was used only on gauze-like clothing fabrics. In Laos, Thailand, and Burma, peasants embroidered geometric patterns in reds and pinks on black clothing. Uzbeks used cross stitch for intricate geometric patterns for dowry hangings and bedspreads, rather than clothing. In the nineteenth century, these were made for sale and soon became collectors' pieces. The Bedouins of the Middle East worked stylized floral designs on silk and cotton for long wedding dresses to be worn with ornate headgear and jewelry. Ornate variations of cross stitch were probably

introduced to Spain and Portugal by the invading Moors in the Middle Ages. There are similarities of design in cross stitch that was traditionally worked in Spain, Italy, and Greece and in Morocco.

Cross-stitch embroidery has also played a role in the rituals and religions of many countries. It was often used for church hangings, and embroidered articles of clothing were made for life's major events, especially birth and marriage. In Spain, for example, linen shirts would be embroidered for the bridegroom with red cross stitch initials just below the neck opening.

European cross stitch, which forms the mainstay of the projects in this book, became established during the sixteenth century. It was very much an activity for the rich and leisured, such as courtly ladies, and was one of the

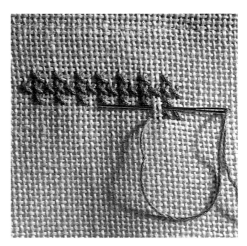

earliest accomplishments that they expected their daughters to learn. In western Europe, for many centuries, peasants were prevented by sumptuary laws from decorating their costume, although gradually the art of embroidery spread into even the poorest homes.

Soon cross stitch was used to ornament functional items of clothing and household linens, throughout Europe. Articles were often embroidered with family initials in red, mainly for washing identification, much as laundries mark items today. Linens were often handed down the family, usually through the female line.

A beautiful antique sampler from the Heimatmuseum in Davos, Switzerland, with a variety of alphabets and a charming collection of flowers and symbols. The pinkish-red cotton is typical of the region, although it has faded somewhat with the years. Pieces like this are indicative of the embroiderer's skill.

Red thread is very widely used in European embroidery. This is an echo of early people's use of red ocher, and of sealing contracts with blood. Red also symbolizes life, love, and vitality.

Cross stitch pieces that were entirely decorative include samplers and, occasionally, wall hangings or bed drapes. Samplers are, as their name implies, samples of embroidery: practice pieces created by young girls to develop their embroidery skills. They were invariably worked on linen fabric and used threads in various colored silks, plus gold and silver. Some samplers were remarkably intricate, using many different stitches including cross stitch. However, cross stitch became the predominant form of embroidery, probably because of its simplicity.

The earliest known British sampler, dated 1598, was made by a Jane Bostake and is now in the Victoria and Albert Museum in London, England. There are others from about the same period in private collections, but unfortunately their embroiderers did not date their work so helpfully. Samplers remained a popular form of embroidery right through the Victorian era and into the present century.

Mass production of textiles in the twentieth century brought about a sharp decline in the popularity of embroidery generally for several decades in Britain. But in the U.S., embroidery remained popular, and indeed ornate Victorian and simpler Shaker styles are even more popular today. Samplers are still a wonderful way to learn cross stitch and to make a special heirloom, while tablecloths, book covers, pillow covers, and other items are satisfying to make and have in the home.

Like many other crafts, cross stitch is currently enjoying a great revival as many people turn back to traditional pastimes for recreation. Embroidery is certainly a therapeutic activity, and cross stitch in particular is easy to master, relying only on neatness and accurate planning to produce simple but pleasing designs.

As the projects in this book show, cross stitch appeals to a range of abilities. Learners can try the simple sachets, box lids or table napkins, while experienced embroiderers will be rewarded by more challenging projects such as tablecloths, bed linen or drapes. Whatever your level of expertise, the following pages are filled with a whole host of traditional designs that will bring delight for years to come.

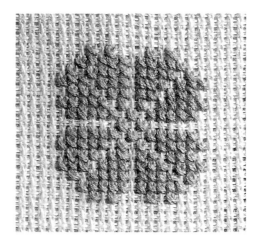

TOP An example of linen woven expressly for embroidery. It has a loose weave with highly visible holes for easy counting and plotting.

ABOVE Tightly stitched letters on a fine hand-loomed linen give the impression of scrolled letters. Such detail would be impossible to achieve on a looser weave.

Before You Begin

The various projects in this book vary considerably in the level of skill required, from the Pincushion Boxes (page 123) and Lavender Sachets (page 118) to the very complex tasseled cloth (page 62). For all these projects, however, some basic rules and requirements apply.

BASIC SEWING REQUIREMENTS
These include:

    Embroidery scissors
    Fabric, thread, needle
    Good light source
    Clean and dry hands.

FABRICS FOR CROSS STITCH

Cross stitch is a very methodical pastime. Its art is not merely in a nicely formed stitch, but in the plotting of the pattern and counting the stitches.

It is necessary to work on a material that has an even weave: that is, a fabric that contains the same number of threads over a given distance, both vertically and horizontally. The threads are counted, in order to work over one, two or more threads, according to the fineness of the stitches and the thickness of the embroidery thread.

Evenweave fabrics come in many varieties, but are graded by the number of threads per inch. The most common, basic cloth used for cross stitching is called Aida. It comes in many thread counts and colors and is woven in such a way that the holes are very clear and even, to allow easy plotting and stitching. (Complete beginners or children might prefer to try a cloth called Herta, which has an even bolder and larger weave.)

Linen was the most commonly used fabric for the items in this book. They are mostly antique pieces, and the work of accomplished needle-women. While linen is very practical for household items, it may be easier to work on a fabric with a guaranteed thread count.

Therefore, as an alternative, purpose-made embroidery fabrics, with suitable thread counts, have been specified for each project. While these are more costly than ordinary fabric, they are helpful for the less-experienced embroiderer. They are described in counts, such as 14-count, 28-count, etc., which refer to the number of threads per inch.

It will become obvious, from the directions for each project in the following pages, how many threads should be taken up per stitch. For example: 14 stitches per inch on a 28-count fabric will require two threads per stitch.

RIGHT A colorful floral border in progress. The pattern is centered between the two brown woven lines with the use of a running stitch, shown in red.

TOP AND MIDDLE *Crisp linen depicting red hearts, in progress and completed.*

BELOW *A snowflake embroidered onto a cotton tea towel fabric.*

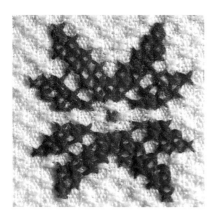

An additional advantage of these fabrics, especially for the beginner, is that when new, they are reasonably stiff. The stiffness disappears with handling, but can be reinstated if the fabric is ironed.

Don't let these specifications prevent you from trying some other fine linens and cottons, but do make sure they can be laundered easily. The effect of linen is very stunning and worth the extra work it takes to count and work evenly. In fact, almost any cloth can be cross stitched once you become proficient.

The size of fabric needed for each project has been measured to provide plenty of room for the cross stitch design, so that if any slight variations in the size of the embroidery itself occur, there should be additional cloth on which to accommodate it. Once the entire piece is finished, the fabric can be trimmed to the correct size before being hemmed.

EMBROIDERY THREAD

There are many types of thread available for embroidery, varying from silks to synthetics. It is fun to experiment with different ones, but for uniformity and simplicity stranded cotton floss has been specified for the projects in this book.

Stranded floss, as its name implies, is made of six strands of cotton thread, twisted together. It comes in a large array of good colors, is easy to separate, and is colorfast. Before starting to stitch, you should separate the six strands into single ones, and then re-combine them into the required number, as listed in the directions.

Colors are given in the two commonly available brands: Anchor and DMC.

NEEDLES

Tapestry needles should be used for cross stitch, as these somewhat blunt-ended needles pass through the fabric without splitting or fraying it. Needle sizes range from 20 to 26, and the correct size for each project is specified in the directions.

CROSS STITCH TECHNIQUE

An experienced cross stitch embroiderer will always judge a piece, not by the front but by the neatness and evenness of the back.

There are two ways of sewing a cross stitch. The first is to work a row of half stitches, then work back over it with the other half. The second is to make rows of whole stitches. Generally, when working a large block of stitches in one color, it is fastest to work the first method. If you have a more complex and multicolored pattern, then follow the latter. The most important thing to remember is that the top part of the stitch should always slant in the same direction on any piece of work, or it will look untidy.

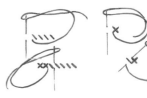

When starting a thread, never knot the ends. It makes the work lumpy, and with age, the knots pull through the holes. Leave a length of thread at the back and after finishing with a length, work the ends into the back.

PLOTTING A DESIGN

To plot out a design, two things must be done. First, cut a piece of cloth slightly larger than required (as suggested in the directions) and fold it in half vertically. Using an ordinary running or basting stitch, sew a line down the middle. Repeat this for a horizontal line. This will be your main guide for plotting the pattern. Where patterns are repeated with a "mirror" image, use the same logical folding method to plot the various repeats.

Then, using the chart as a guide, count the stitches, working over the desired number of threads.

Second, always work from the middle outward. You won't find you've suddenly run out of fabric after days of embroidery.

Where a motif appears in isolation, you may wish to use a basting thread (or even a special marking pen that disappears in the first wash) to mark out the position of the motif.

FINISHING TOUCHES

Once a piece has been finished, it may look slightly uneven from stretching while sewing. Simply lay it face down, cover with a damp cloth, and iron it gently until it is even. Do not iron the front, as it will flatten the stitches and reduce the charm of the embroidery.

Certain stitches have been suggested in the finishing directions for an authentic, traditional finish. These include:

SLIPSTITCH

This stitch is used for an almost invisible finish on hems.

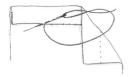

Slide the needle through the folded edge and at the same place, pick up a thread of the under fabric. Continue, spacing stitches ⅛–¼ inch apart.

HERRINGBONE STITCH

Worked like cross stitch, but the stitches are overlapped at their ends, rather than in the middle.

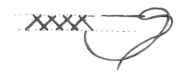

BLANKET STITCH

Gives a decorative finish to a hem. Work from left to right between two lines. Bring the needle up on the lower line and hold the thread down. Insert the needle on the upper line and push through to the lower line. Draw the needle through the loop, and pull the thread taut. Repeat.

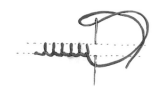

HEMSTITCH

A decorative method of anchoring a hem, using drawn threads.

1 Pull out two threads along the stitching line. Turn the hem up to the edge of the drawn threads.

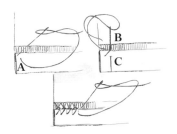

2 Bring the needle through at A, through the hem. Take the thread to

the right, then pointing the needle toward the left, pass it under and over two or three fabric threads (use the same number each time). Pull through and with the needle perpendicular, insert at B and bring through to the front of the material at C, on a line where the thread first came up. Repeat.

HOW TO MITER A CORNER

1 On each raw edge, turn over a small amount of fabric, wrong sides together. (Exact measurements are given for each project.) Press. Turn over a slightly larger amount and press well, especially at the corners. Pin the hem to within 3 inches of each corner.

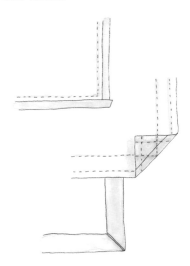

2 Unfold each corner, and fold the corner of the fabric up so that there is an exact diagonal at the point of the corner. Press. Unfold and trim the fabric near the diagonal fold.

3 Turn the diagonal over along the pressed line, then fold each side back up along its pressing lines to form a neat mitered corner. Pin in place, then slipstitch the hem.

Samplers

Alphabet Sampler

This German sampler, dated 1891, is a fine example of accomplished embroidery. Samplers were stitched by beginners as practice for embroidery techniques, and the alphabet was traditionally used for such a purpose. The greater the skill, the more varied were the styles of letter. Here there are several different alphabets, some using two-colored letters, some surrounded by a pretty border or pattern.

Today, samplers provide both decoration and admirable examples of past skills. Modern or period samplers can be enjoyed and preserved for posterity by framing – but should be hung out of the sun, so that they do not fade.

If you are just beginning cross stitch and would prefer a simpler piece, use just one or two of the styles. Make sure that you plot out the letters before you start, so you have a well-planned piece to frame when finished. The following charts show the letters on this particular sampler, but throughout the book there are various other letters, any of which can be adapted to personalize your own piece.

Linen was the usual base fabric for samplers, as its threads are even and distinct. Usually, the finer the linen, the more accomplished the piece looks, but of course, it is more demanding on the eyesight to cross stitch onto fine linen.

RIGHT A colorful sampler showing a tremendous variety of alphabet styles.
ABOVE A detail of a lovely two-toned script.

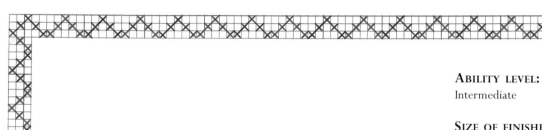

Colors:

		DMC	Anchor
■	Red	321	9046
■	Dark blue	3750	123

Two tone letters:

■	Beige	437	362
■	Pale blue	519	167

Two tone letters:

■	Pink	899	40
■	Taupe	640	393

Two tone letters:

■	Brown	838	380
■	Pale blue	519	167

	Two tone:	DMC	Anchor
■	Pale blue	519	167
■	Dark blue	3750	123
■	Pink scroll	899	40

Multicolored letters:

■	Red	321	9046
■	Blue	930	922
■	Light blue	519	167
■	Taupe	640	393
■	Orange	676	891
■	Light Gray	318	399
■	Pink	758	868
■	Beige	841	378

ABILITY LEVEL:
Intermediate

SIZE OF FINISHED STITCHED AREA:
25 ½ x 15 inches
Size of top row capital letters:
⅞ inch

NUMBER OF STITCHES PER INCH:
13

STRANDED COTTON EMBROIDERY FLOSS:
2 strands

NEEDLE SIZE:
24/26

FABRIC:
28 x 16 inches cream linen, or
Zweigart 27-count Linda 1235
(Cotton, Color no. 264)

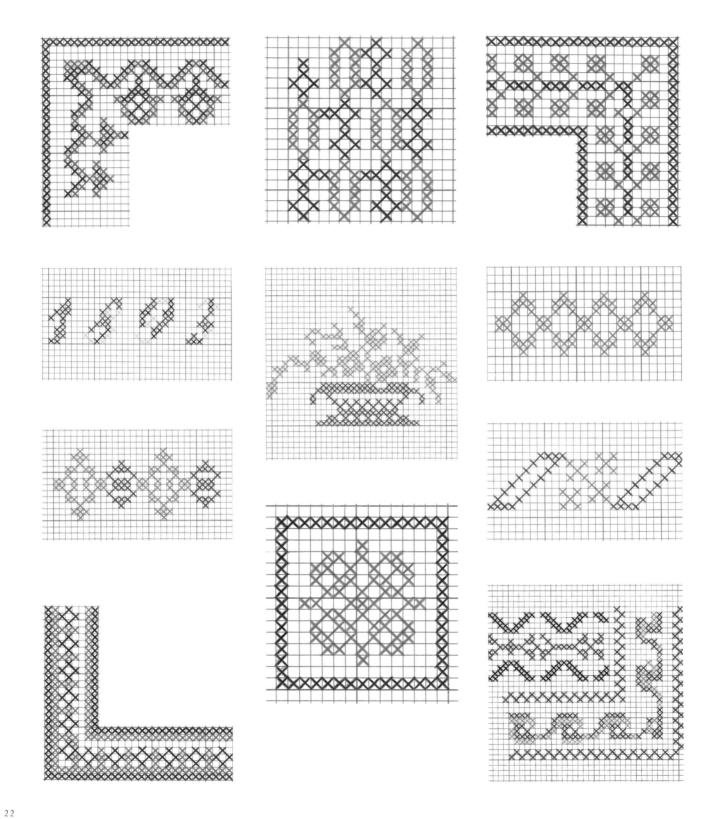

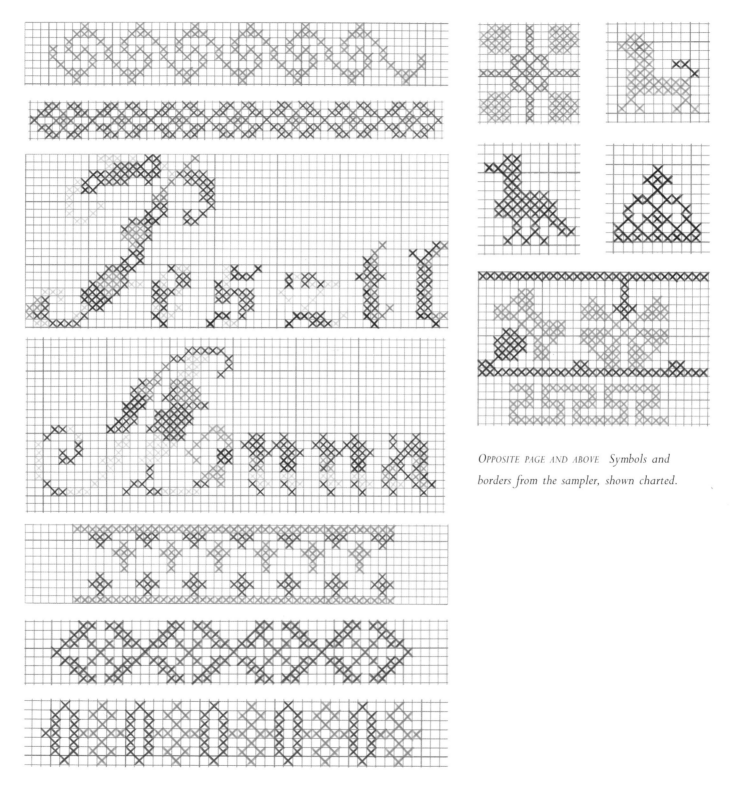

OPPOSITE PAGE AND ABOVE Symbols and borders from the sampler, shown charted.

Grace Shaw 1815

Grace Shaw Sampler

Samplers are records not only of needlecraft quality, but of the person who made them. They often bear the needlewoman's name or initials, some indication of her family history, and the year in which she made it. Also stitched in are pictures of houses, garden flowers, animals, and household items. Religious symbols, short prayers, and biblical quotations were also sometimes employed.

This sampler dates back to 1816 and was made by a Grace Shaw, almost certainly in England. It is charmingly simple and decorative, with a multicolored alphabet, a simple house with flowers sprouting from a chimney flanked by a pair of flower baskets. The red and green border is a typical feature of samplers. Borders frame a piece of work and make it look more complete. They vary tremendously in pattern, and several are featured in this book that could be adapted for a sampler. Make sure that you either work the border from the middle of a line, or count very carefully so that the corners line up with each other.

Although it looks complicated, this sampler is fairly easy to make and looks very impressive with its variety of color. As with any counted cross stitch project, plotting and planning are important for the overall result of the work. If you wish to substitute different letters or decorative motifs, there are many other examples in this book.

LEFT Handwoven natural-coloured linen, beautifully stitched into a sampler.
ABOVE A detail, showing a basket of fruit.

COLORS:

	DMC	Anchor
Light Gray	822	390
Dark Gray	535	273
Light Green	3364	260
Green	895	269
Pale Pink	3688	66
Wine	3685	69
Red	347	13
Light Brown	433	371
Blue	3750	123

ABILITY LEVEL:
Intermediate

SIZE OF FINISHED STITCHED
AREA: 17 ¼ x 10 inches

NUMBER OF STITCHES PER INCH:
18

STRANDED COTTON EMBROIDERY
FLOSS: 1 strand

NEEDLE SIZE: 24/26

FABRIC:
19 x 12 inches fine ecru linen, or
Zweigart 18-count Fine Aida (Cotton,
Color no. 13); 18-count Floba 1198
(Rayon/Linen, Color no. 53);
36-count Edinborough 3217 (Linen,
Color no. 222)

House Sampler

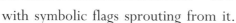

Another fine sampler, English in origin, this one dates back to 1845, and shows a grand castle or home. The many windows are distinctive architecturally, looking somewhat Elizabethan. The sampler possibly depicts, or is based on, the royal palace of Hampton Court, near London, England.

There are heraldic-looking birds atop the many little roofs. The sampler has a pretty, ornately stylized floral border in soft green and red. On one side of the central tower, there is a large flower in the same colors, while the other side of the tower has a more formal urn with symbolic flags sprouting from it.

The plotting of this sampler will be crucial, as it isn't as symmetrical as it appears.

Once you have accomplished this piece of work, you may wish to frame it yourself. However, before you try to mount it make sure that it is properly ironed. Always use acid-free mounting boards, and center the pattern carefully. The best way of attaching the cloth to the card is first to pin the piece evenly around the edge, miter and stitch down the corners, and then lace it in position using strong thread. This will hold the sampler in place when you place the glass and frame on it.

RIGHT   An intricately cross stitched sampler is appealing in its heavy, dark frame.
ABOVE   A detail of the roof, portraying heraldic birds.

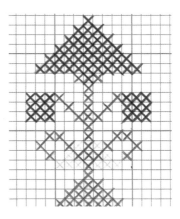

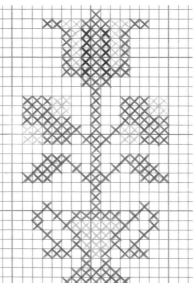

ABILITY LEVEL: Advanced

SIZE OF FINISHED STITCHED AREA: 17 ½ inches square

NUMBER OF STITCHES PER INCH: 12

STRANDED COTTON EMBROIDERY FLOSS: 2 strands

NEEDLE SIZE: 24/26

FABRIC:
22-inch square fine cream linen or cotton, or Zweigart 25-count Lugana 3835 (Cotton/Rayon, Color no. 264); 36-count Edinborough 3217 (Linen, Color no. 101).

COLORS:

		DMC	Anchor
	Red	355	341
	Blue	930	922
	Khaki Green	371	855
	Stone	3032	903
	Rose	3778	9575
	Beige	612	832
	Dark Brown	3371	382
	Gray	453	231
	Light Brown	841	378
	Pink	224	893

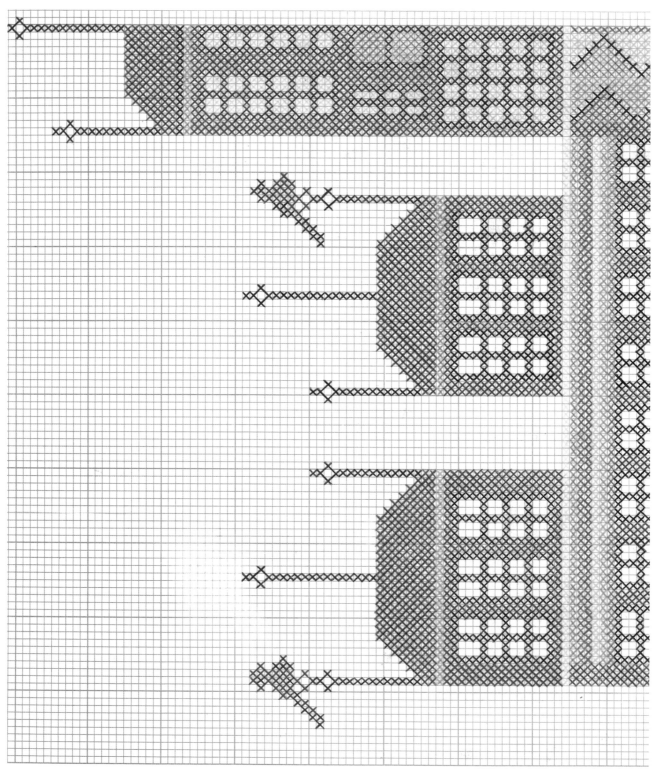

←— Top

Illustration overlaps 11 lines

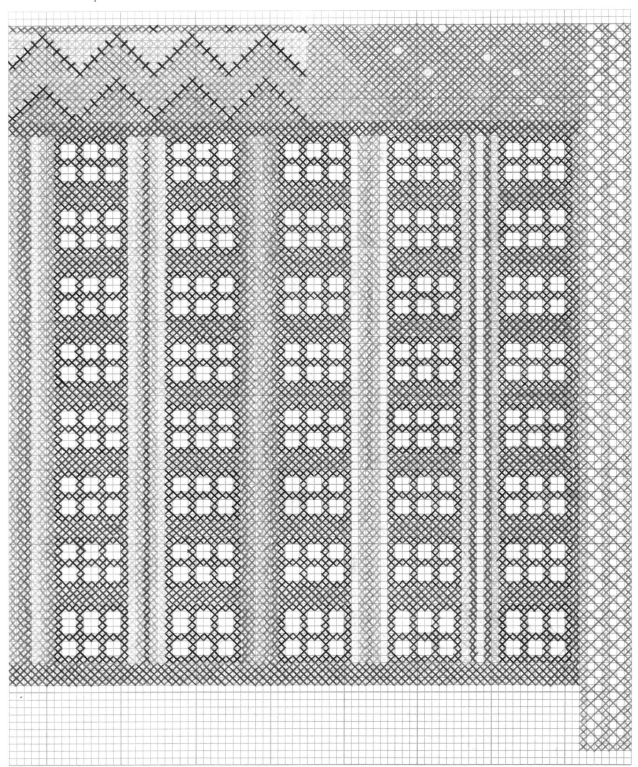

← *Top*

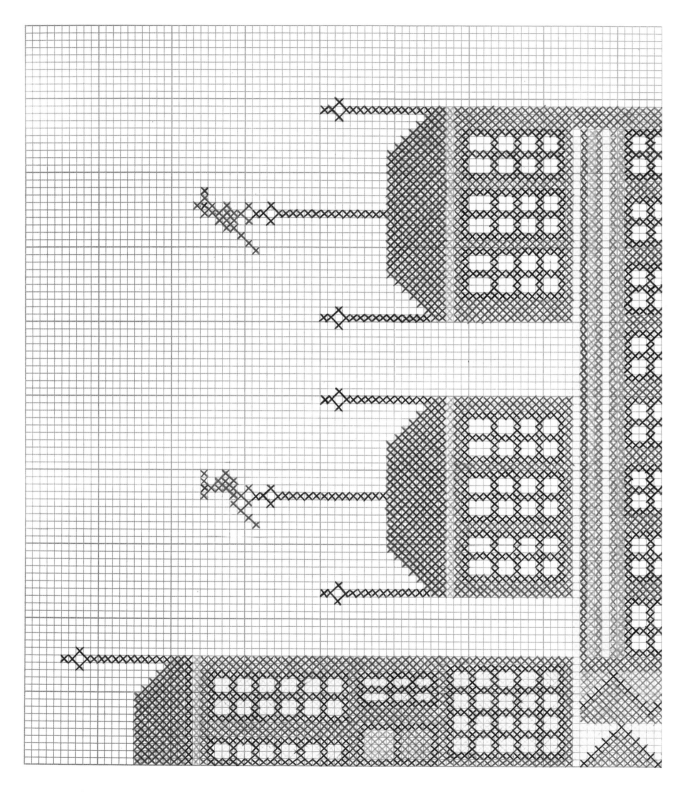

← *Top*

Illustration overlaps 11 lines

← *Top*

Table Linen

Margreth
Valär.
1843.

Napkins & Napkin Rings

Table napkins in Britain and Europe date back to the fifteenth century where they developed in the highest social circles. At first, a large tablecloth was spread over the table, and diners would wipe their hands and mouths on the long sides. Gradually, individual pieces of cloth were introduced for this purpose (mainly woven damask and linen), and the custom of separate napkins soon took hold. Napkin rings are not as common now as they used to be, but in Europe people used to have their own personalized ring, for easy identification and to save on laundering. Napkin rings make lovely gifts, especially if they are embroidered with details such as the recipient's initials.

The motifs shown here are all easy to sew and would make ideal starter projects for children. The heart and house are adaptable to many cloth types; we show it on a cheerful gingham check.

LEFT Woven cotton gingham looks charming with these embroidered motifs. The heart and schoolhouse are well-known Shaker symbols.
ABOVE AND RIGHT A leaf and a kettle are easy for beginners.

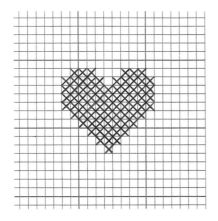

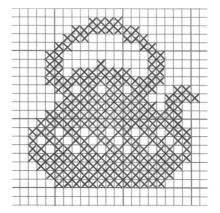

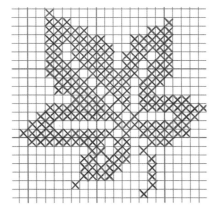

Napkins

ABILITY LEVEL: Beginner

SIZE OF FINISHED NAPKIN:
20 ½ inches square

SIZE OF HEART MOTIF:
1 ¾ x 1 ½ inches

**NUMBER OF STITCHES PER
INCH:** 8, 12 (house)

**STRANDED COTTON
EMBROIDERY FLOSS:** 4 strands

NEEDLE SIZE: 22/24

FABRIC:
21-inch square red cotton check (or
plain linen)

TO FINISH
1 Make a hem all around by turning
over ¼ inch, then another ½ inch to the
wrong side. Miter the corners (see
page 15) and pin.

2 Machine stitch and press well.

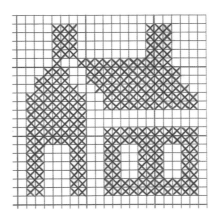

COLORS:

		DMC	Anchor			DMC	Anchor
	Red	321	9046	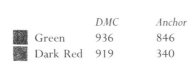	Green	936	846
	Black	310	403		Dark Red	919	340

Napkin rings

ABILITY LEVEL: Beginner

SIZE OF FINISHED CROSS STITCH PANEL: 6 ¼ x 1 inch

NUMBER OF STITCHES PER INCH: 9

STRANDED COTTON EMBROIDERY FLOSS: 3 strands

NEEDLE SIZE: 24

FABRIC:
Strip of open-weave white linen or cotton, 2 inches wide, with edges turned under ½ inch, or white Zweigart Aida Band, 1 inch wide

OTHER MATERIALS:
Wooden napkin ring, 2 inches in diameter, or stiffener such as buckram

TO FINISH

1 If you are using plain fabric, turn over ½ inch to the wrong side along each edge. Press.

2 Wrap the fabric or strip around the napkin ring, trim to fit, and secure with fabric glue.

3 Hand stitch the ends of the strip closed.

COLORS:

		DMC	Anchor
■	Red	321	9046
■	Blue	797	132

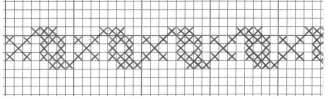

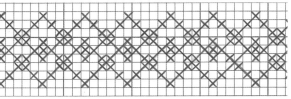

Table Mats

If you are new to cross stitch, a small table mat or placemat is one of the simplest pieces to start with and is always a welcome decorative addition in any home. Why not embroider a set of placemats for your dining table, or an occasional mat as a gift for a friend? Smaller pieces are easy to plot and soon completed. A set of table mats with matching napkins would make a lovely wedding present.

For ease of laundering, it is recommended that the mats are made on the best, quality linen, as it washes beautifully and has a natural lustre that adds a touch of class to any table.

We show several traditional designs from the Graubünden area of eastern Switzerland. Red and dark pink were the most commonly used colors in this area, but you can substitute any color to complement your china or the room.

The placemats used in the table setting (pages 44-7) are part of a set of eight that I embroidered while a young schoolgirl in Switzerland. It is a simple design to stitch, yet its heart motifs are charming and attractive.

The small square mat with the candlestick on it (page 48) looks very stylish if trimmed with braid, stitching, or crochet in red and white, or a color to match the cross stitch.

The gingham mat (page 49) is very easy to make; instead of counting threads, you simply stitch on alternate squares.

RIGHT Embroidered table mats lend themselves particularly well to old wooden tables. Here, the linen mats are bordered on each side with a heart motif in cheerful red that can still be seen when a plate is in position on the mat.

Four-heart border placemat

ABILITY LEVEL:
Beginner

SIZE OF FINISHED MAT:
14 x 12 inches

WIDTH OF BORDER:
3⅛ inches

CENTRAL GAP BETWEEN BORDERS:
6¼ inches

NUMBER OF STITCHES PER INCH:
11

**STRANDED COTTON EMBROIDERY
FLOSS:** 3 strands

NEEDLE SIZE: 24

FABRIC:
15 x 13 inches medium-weight white
linen, or Zweigart
11-count Pearl Aida 1007 (Cotton,
Color no. 1); 22-count Hardanger
1008 (Cotton, Color no. 1)

TO FINISH
1 Turn ¼ inch to the wrong side
around each edge of the fabric, then
another ¼ inch. Miter the corners (see
page 15) and pin.

2 Slipstitch in place (see page 15).

COLORS:

		DMC	Anchor
■	Red	321	9046

*Simple placemat with
narrow border*
ABILITY LEVEL:
Beginner

SIZE OF FINISHED MAT:
16 ½ x 12 ¾ inches

WIDTH OF BORDER: 1inch

**DISTANCE FROM MIDDLE OF
EMBROIDERED STRIP TO HEMMED
EDGE:** 1 ⅝ inches

NUMBER OF STITCHES PER INCH:
14

**STRANDED COTTON EMBROIDERY
FLOSS:** 2 strands

COLORS:

		DMC	Anchor
▨	Red	321	9046

NEEDLE SIZE: 24/26

FABRIC:
17 ¼ x 13 ½ inches medium-weight
cream or white linen or Zweigart 28-
count fabrics: Pastel linen 3234
(Color no. 12); Quaker cloth 3993
(Linen/Cotton, Color no. 101);
Jubilee 3232 (Cotton, Color no. 1).

TO FINISH
1 Turn ¼ inch to the wrong side
around each edge of the fabric, then
another ⅝ inch. Miter the corners (see
page 15) and pin.

2 Slipstitch in place, or hemstitch, as
in the original (see page 15).

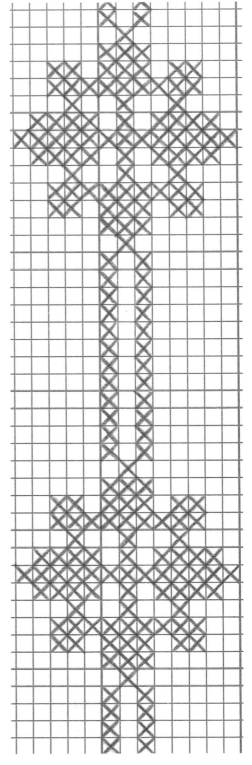

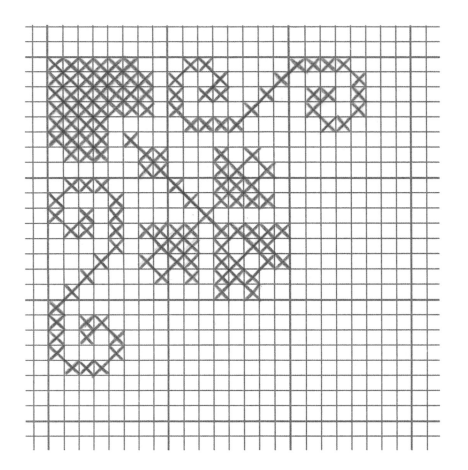

Square candlestick mat

ABILITY LEVEL:
Beginner

SIZE OF FINISHED MAT:
7 inches square

NUMBER OF STITCHES PER INCH:
12

STRANDED COTTON EMBROIDERY FLOSS: 3 strands

NEEDLE SIZE:
24/26

FABRIC:
8-inch square medium-weight white linen, or Zweigart 25-count Lugana 3835 (Cotton/Rayon, Color no. 100)

TO FINISH

1 Machine overlock or blanket stitch a square of 7 inches (see page 15). Trim edges.

2 Finish with decorative braid, if desired.

COLORS:

		DMC	Anchor
■	Red	321	9046

Gingham mat

ABILITY LEVEL: Beginner

SIZE OF FINISHED MAT (WITHOUT LACE EDGING): 12 ½ inches square

SIZE OF ONE CHECK: ¼ inch

NUMBER OF STITCHES PER INCH: 5 (or number dictated by squares on gingham)

STRANDED COTTON EMBROIDERY FLOSS: 6 strands

NEEDLE SIZE: 22

FABRIC: 13-inch square checked gingham cotton

OTHER MATERIALS: 1½ yards lace, ½-inch wide

TO FINISH

1 Turn ¼ inch to the wrong side around each edge of the fabric, then another ¼ inch. Miter the corners (see page 15) and pin.

2 Slipstitch in place (see page 15). Sew on lace, if desired.

COLORS:

	DMC	Anchor
Red	321	9046

Rose Tablecloth

Flowers and embroidery have gone hand-in-hand for centuries, and this classical rose-embroidered cloth is simple and pretty. The way the colors have been used here, to create an illusion of depth and shadow, is very typical of Danish cross stitch. It has a

more painterly effect than the solid blocks of color typical of Eastern European work. The roses are joined together with wavy lines of flattened cross stitch. This is similar to traditional, square cross stitch but the width of the stitch is two to three times the height, giving it an elongated shape. We show this as square cross stitch in the charts, but you could change it to an elongated stitch, if preferred.

The origin of this particular cloth is unknown, but it was bought in Derbyshire, England. It is a very fine cotton weave, one of the more difficult cloths on which to cross stitch as the fine threads are hard to count. Plotting the design looks easier than it is. Map it out by laying the hemmed cloth on the floor and mark the roses first, using tailor's chalk. Then outline them in basting stitches for a more permanent marking.

It is possible to achieve just as effective a look by using a custom-made 20-count embroidery fabric, taking in two threads per stitch.

RIGHT This tablecloth, although not typical of the regional embroidery, looks completely at home in an old, traditional Swiss kitchen.
ABOVE Detail of the beautiful rose motif.

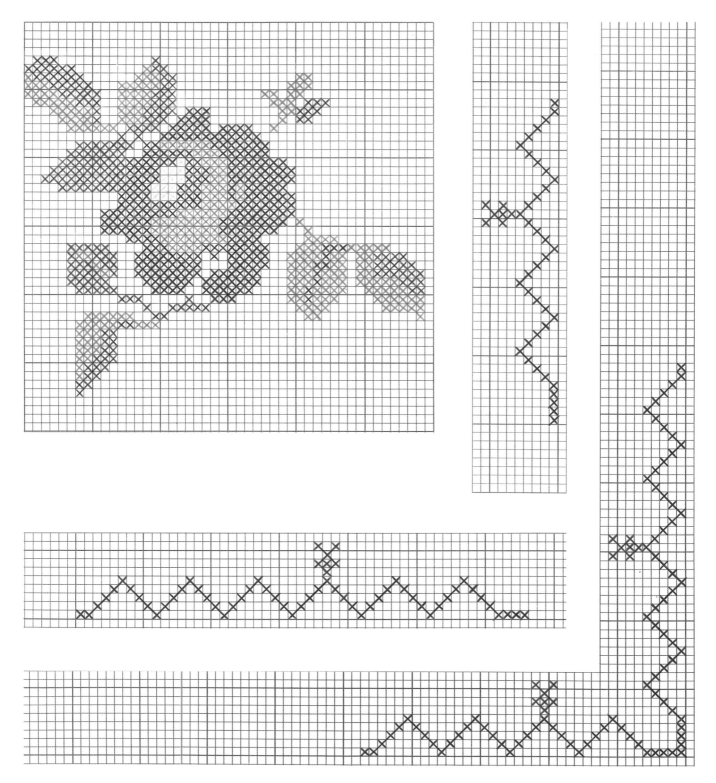

ABILITY LEVEL:
Intermediate

SIZE OF FINISHED TABLECLOTH:
52 ½ inches square

NUMBER OF STITCHES PER INCH: 10

STRANDED COTTON EMBROIDERY FLOSS: 3 strands

NEEDLE SIZE: 24

FABRIC:
53-inch square medium-weight white cotton or linen, or Zweigart 20-count 3256 Valerie (Cotton/Rayon, Color no. 100).

TO FINISH

1 Turn ¼ inch to the wrong side around each edge of the fabric, then another ½ inch. Miter the corners (see page 15) and pin on the right side of the cloth.

2 Work flattened cross stitch right around the right side of the tablecloth so that it anchors the hem neatly in place instead of ordinary hemming.

COLORS:

	DMC	Anchor
Red	666	46
Dark red	221	897
Pink	962	75
Dark green	890	683
Light green	703	239
Dark blue	797	132
Yellow	307	289

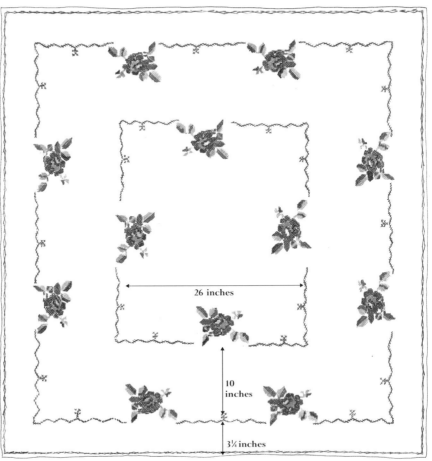

Carnation Tablecloth

This is a charming and rather naive tablecloth that one of my sisters gave me for Christmas, knowing my passion for cross stitch, especially in red. Its edges are finished with blanket stitch using the same embroidery thread. Red was a predominant color for cross stitch in many countries. There is a tremendous vitality

in the strength of color. However, strong red is not to everyone's taste, so why not make the cloth in a pretty pale blue, or a chic black?

The carnation motif appears in cross stitched embroidery the world over, being a symbol of fertility. As many cloths in years gone by were embroidered for wedding trousseaus, this isn't altogether surprising. The pattern of this cloth divides into four equal parts, so that once you have mastered one corner the rest should fall into place quite easily, making a beautiful showcase for your work.

As with all table linen, make sure that you use a good-quality cloth that can be laundered frequently at high temperatures. Also hem the edges well to prevent fraying during laundering. As most embroidery cottons are colorfast, you shouldn't have a problem with colors running, but do double check before buying the embroidery thread.

LEFT A bold, blanket-stitched edge gives this cloth a definite border.
ABOVE The main motif of the cloth that is repeated in each corner.

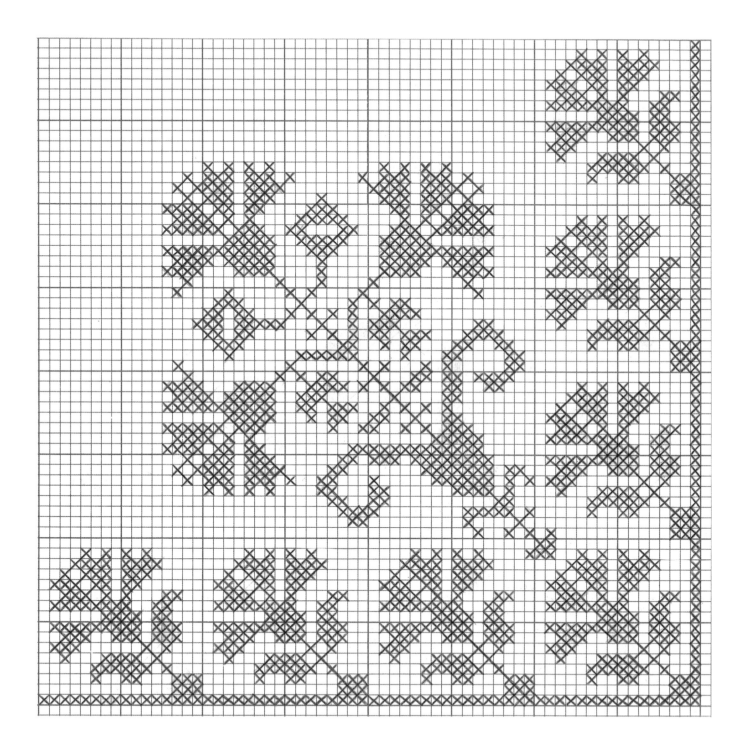

ABILITY LEVEL:
Intermediate

SIZE OF FINISHED TABLECLOTH:
27 inches square

**NUMBER OF STITCHES PER
INCH:** 6

**STRANDED COTTON EMBROIDERY
FLOSS:** 6 strands

NEEDLE SIZE: 22

FABRIC:
28 ½ inch square white or cream
heavy cotton or linen, or
Zweigart 18-count fabrics: Fine
Aida 3793 (Cotton, Color no.
400); Davosa 3770 (Cotton,
Color no. 264)

TO FINISH
1 Press the cloth so that it is
even and square. On each side,
measure out 2 ¾ inches from the
edge of the embroidery, and
trim.

2 Turn ½ inch to the wrong side
around each edge of the fabric,
then another ½ inch. Miter the
corners (see page 15) and pin,
then machine stitch with thread
matching the fabric.

3 Using the same color and
number of strands as the cross
stitch, work right around the
hem in blanket stitch, spacing
the stitches about ¼ inch apart
(see page 15).

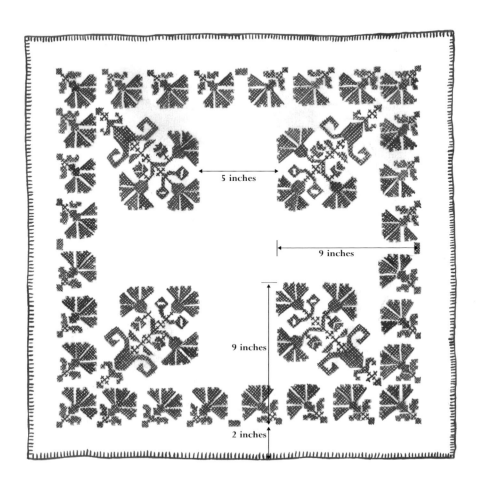

5 inches

9 inches

9 inches

2 inches

COLORS:

		DMC	Anchor
▨	Red	321	9046

Peacock Tablecloth

This cheerful yellow peacock cloth was found in London, but it is doubtful that it was embroidered in England. It looks as if it might have been made in Germany or Austria.

There are two stylized peacocks facing each other at each corner, with three sunbursts between them. The checkerboard pattern on the bodies of the peacocks represents their multi-

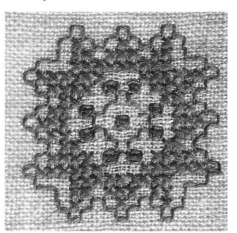

colored plumage, and the outspread feathers are portrayed as crude arrows of red and blue. Peacocks have been used in embroidery as a sacred symbol for centuries and appear all over the world on clothing and ceremonial pieces. They symbolize beauty, dignity, and sometimes royalty.

It is rare to find cross stitch embroidered on anything but white or cream cloth, but it looks very fetching on this yellow. However, if yellow linen is difficult or impossible to find, it will look just as attractive on a more neutral color.

The edging on this cloth is fine drawn, thread-work that is probably the work of the embroiderer. It is lovely to be able to finish off a piece of work in such fine detail, so if you wish to use the same sort of finish on the hem, follow the directions on page 15 for hemstitching.

LEFT   The stylized corner motifs on this cloth are displayed to good effect on a small table that allows them to hang down.
ABOVE   A detail of one of the three sunburst motifs on the cloth.

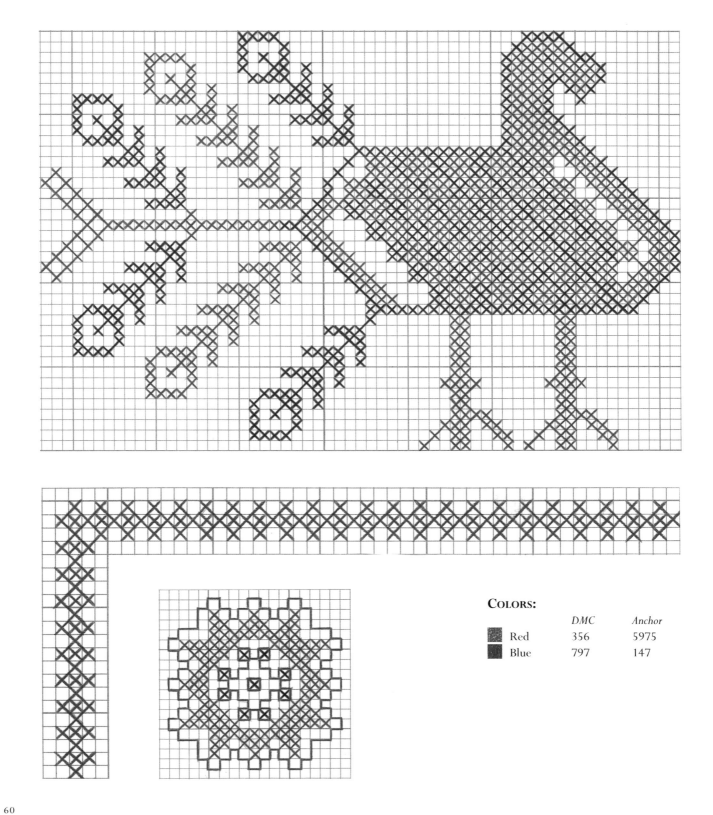

COLORS:

		DMC	Anchor
	Red	356	5975
	Blue	797	147

ABILITY LEVEL: Intermediate

SIZE OF FINISHED CLOTH:
34 inches square

SIZE OF PEACOCK:
4 x 6 ¼ inches

SIZE OF STARBURST:
1 ¾ inches square

DISTANCE FROM OUTER TO INNER BORDERS OF CROSS STITCH: 5 inches

NUMBER OF STITCHES PER INCH: 10

STRANDED COTTON EMBROIDERY FLOSS: 3 strands

NEEDLE SIZE: 24

FABRIC:
42-inch square yellow linen, or Zweigart 20-count Valerie 3256 (Cotton/Rayon Color no. 307 light brown, or 264, cream; yellow not available in suitable Zweigart fabric)

TO FINISH
1 Press the cloth flat and even. Trim the edges of the cloth to leave a border all around, 2 inches from the outer edge of the cross stitch border.

2 Measure ¾ inch out from the edge of the cross stitch border, and fold the remainder over, wrong sides together. Press. Miter the corners (see page 15).

3 Make a ¼-inch hem on the wrong side, and slipstitch in place. Alternatively, finish with hemstitch – as on the original. (See page 15 for techniques.)

Fringed Tablecloth

This complex but highly decorative linen tablecloth was probably made in eastern Switzerland, using the traditional local colors, pinkish red and powder blue.

Linen used to be woven specially for all sorts of household uses: narrow widths for towels, and different, wider widths for

tablecloths. Some fabrics would consist of narrow strips of colored linen interspersed with wider bands of cream linen. An embroiderer would then design her own pattern in the bands. Many shops in Austria, Germany, and Switzerland still sell woven cloth similar to this.

The original fabric of this cloth has panels for the cross stitch that look very similar to modern Aida, and the striped borders are in a similar weight but denser cloth. Each motif is bordered with a stitched band, and the whole cloth is edged with knotted fringe. You could reproduce the same effect by using Aida and inserting suitable striped material in between them.

The tasseled fringe adds a sumptuous touch and, if care is taken, is not difficult to make. See the following diagram for a suggestion on knotting.

If you feel that this is too big a project, or you would like a smaller tablecloth, you could use just one motif in the middle and adapt the border to go right around the four edges.

RIGHT A traditional Swiss dining room with rustic, carved pine walls and country chairs offers the ideal setting for this heavy, detailed cloth.
ABOVE A detail of one of the embroidered motifs.

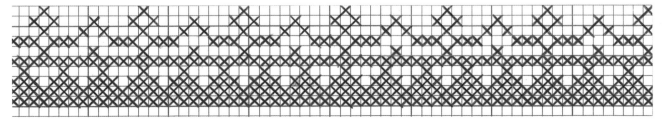

ABILITY LEVEL:
Advanced

SIZE OF FINISHED CLOTH:
56 ¼ x 52 ¾ inches

NUMBER OF STITCHES PER INCH:
8

STRANDED COTTON EMBROIDERY FLOSS: 4 strands

NEEDLE SIZE: 22/24

FABRIC:
Heavy cotton or linen, or
Zweigart 8-count Aida 1006 (Cotton,
Color no. 1), Hertarette 3707
(Cotton, Color no. 1)

OTHER MATERIALS:
Red, blue, and white striped
heavyweight fabric for inserting
between stitched panels.
Matching yarn for knotted fringe

TO FINISH

1 If it is necessary to join panels, use
a ¼ inch seam, and overlock any raw
edges to prevent fraying.

2 Make ¼ inch hems at each edge,
mitering the corners for a smooth
finish (see page 15).

3 Add the knotted fringe over the
hem, if desired.

COLORS:

		DMC	Anchor
	Red	326	59
	Blue	336	149

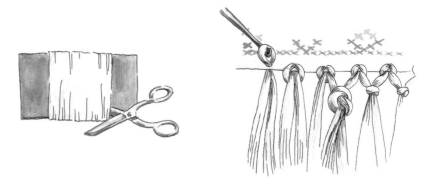

Tasseled Cloth

This very fine cloth, probably from Eastern Europe, must have been embroidered by a highly skilled needlewoman. It has a complex pattern of very small stitches, and the zigzag border with its small tassels is intricately worked.

Although the original stitches are in silk, stranded floss is recommended here. If you wish to substitute silk, remember that silk yarn is rarely colorfast, especially in such a strong color.

This rich, dark linen cloth is embroidered only on three sides, which suggest that it was made for a table that stood against a wall, or perhaps as a wall hanging. It could even have been a church altar cloth.

One thing, however, is certain: it is beautifully embroidered by someone with lots of experience. As with all the more advanced projects in this book, don't try to attempt this unless you have some experience in cross stitching as it could be a very frustrating experience. You could try to adapt the design onto a lower count Aida cloth, thus making a bigger design and therefore a bigger cloth.

The original cloth is finished with tassels on the point of each zigzag. Although they look complicated, these are reasonably easy to make, but it may take a little experimentation to get them to the correct fullness. Once you have made a few, you will then be able to calculate the amount of thread or silk needed.

LEFT This unbleached linen was hand woven and then exquisitely embroidered with fine stitches in a rich-colored silk. The zigzag edge is emphasized and finished with little matching tassels.

ABILITY LEVEL: Advanced

SIZE OF FINISHED CLOTH: 59 x 46 inches
EACH PATTERN REPEAT: 6½ inches square
BORDER WIDTH: 1 inch
DEPTH OF ZIGZAGS: 1½ inch

NUMBER OF STITCHES PER INCH: 14

STRANDED COTTON EMBROIDERY FLOSS: 2 strands (or Anchor Silk Marlitt)

NEEDLE SIZE: 24/26

COLORS:

		DMC	Anchor
▨	Rust	918	1003

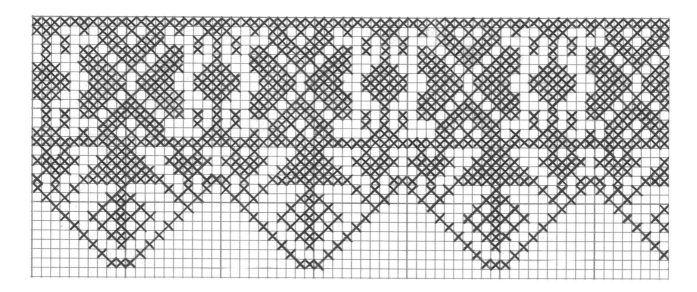

FABRIC:

1¾ yards x 50 inches very fine brown linen, or Zweigart 28-count fabrics: Quaker cloth 3993 (Linen/cotton, Color no. 323), Jubilee 3232 (Cotton, Color no. 372)

OTHER MATERIALS:

Lightweight cotton fabric for zigzag facing

TO FINISH

1 Carefully trim the cloth to give a ⅝-inch border all around the outer zigzag edge of the cross stitch. Do not cut each individual zigzag, but cut the cloth straight, ⅝ inch from the bottom of the points.

2 Cut a piece of facing material to go around the three zigzag sides of the cloth, 3 inches wide. Turn ½ inch over to the wrong side along one raw edge and press.

3 Lay the facing over the zigzags, right sides together. Following the line of the zigzags, pin and baste in position, ⅛ inch out from the edge of the embroidery.

4 Machine stitch along the basting line, and trim the excess material back to ⅛ inch of the stitching. Turn right side out and, using the pointed ends of a pair of scissors, ease out the points. Press.

5 Hem the unembroidered side of the cloth by turning over ¼ inch to the wrong side, and then another ⅛ inch. Pin and slipstitch.

6 Pin the folded edge of the facing to the main cloth, and slipstitch in place.

7 Make a little tassel for each point of the zigzag, using the same colored embroidery thread. Cut a piece of cardboard 3 x 1 inches. Wind thread around the cardboard about 10 or 15 times. Thread a needle with a double strand, pass under the wound threads at one end of the cardboard and tie securely in a knot. Remove the cardboard, and wind the strand tightly around the tassel threads, about ⅜ inches from the top. Slip the needle underneath the wound

portion, and bring it out at the top. Cut the loops at the bottom.

8 Sew a tassel onto each zigzag point.

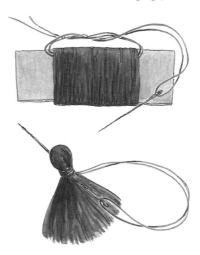

Reindeer Runner

The use of table linen is steeped in tradition. Tablecloths date back to the Middle Ages and were used much as they are today, to protect a table during meals. They were frequently decorated with embroidery, or woven with damask designs.

Before napkins came into use, in about the fifteenth century, a tablecloth was usually covered by a runner which ran the length of the table. This would be used by all and sundry for wiping hands. Luckily, the individual napkin came into vogue, and the table runner was relegated to the way it is used today.

Runners make wonderful showpieces for an embroiderer, with a practical application. They are also useful covers for precious wooden table tops and sideboards, as protection from both scratches and strong sunlight. This rather large runner was probably made in Switzerland, with a very characteristic motif of leaping deer interspersed with heraldic images. Once again, a powerful red makes the images jump out from the background.

The central design is surrounded by a simple border which is inverted on the outside border. Make sure that you plot the design, starting from the middle and working your way out. If you find the cloth too long, take out one or two of the motifs, or even leave off the outside border.

RIGHT This exceptionally long table runner depicts a vigorous hunting scene, embroidered in the ever-popular red thread.

ABOVE A detail showing part of the central panel.

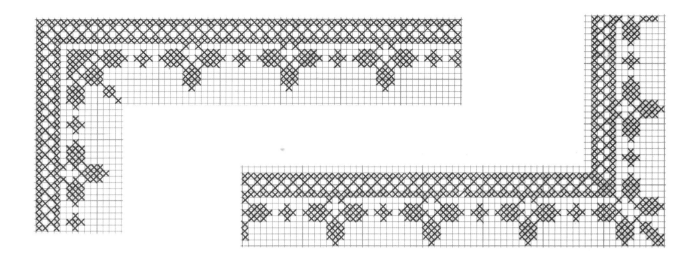

ABILITY LEVEL: Advanced

SIZE OF FINISHED CLOTH:
86 ¼ x 27 ½ inches

NUMBER OF STITCHES PER INCH:
7

STRANDED COTTON EMBROIDERY FLOSS: 4 strands

NEEDLE SIZE: 22/24

FABRIC:
91 x 32 inches heavy cream linen, or Zweigart 14-count Easy Count Aida 3246 (Polyacrylic, Color no. 27) or 28-count Quaker Cloth 3993 (Linen/cotton, Color no. 101)

TO FINISH
1 Press the cloth so that it is square and even. Carefully trim it so that there is ¾ inch of cloth all the way around the outer border.

2 Fold ⅜ inch over, wrong sides together. Press. Then fold another ⅜ inch over to form a hem. Miter the corners carefully (see page 15) and pin.

3 Slipstitch in place using matching thread (see page 15).

COLORS:

		DMC	Anchor
▨	Red	321	9046

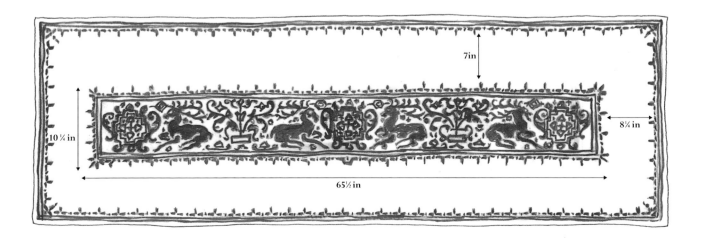

Bed Linen

Sheet & Pillowcase

These beautiful, crisp white cotton sheets have been lovingly and painstakingly embroidered to form part of a very fine wedding trousseau. The lace-edged top sheet has a scroll-like border of stylized carnations (a symbol of fertility) and is interspersed with little flower and animal motifs. The matching white pillowcases are similarly adorned.

The top sheet consists of two pieces of cloth which are buttoned together. The top part has the cross stitched embroidery on it, and the bottom part is plain. The sheet is divided into two parts, linked with buttons, so that the top part need not be laundered as often as the bottom, to preserve the cross stitch for as long as possible. The lace edges were obviously handmade, but as long as preshrunk cotton lace is used, a modern machine-made equivalent would look just as good.

To attempt a project as large and ambitious as this, you need not only time, but also considerable cross stitching experience. This bed linen is made of cotton, but in fact fine linen might be easier to use as it would be clearer to count the threads. Alternatively, you could buy a set of good-quality ready-made sheets or pillowcases, and just add the embroidery to them.

To plot the design, it would be best to use tailor's chalk, then guiding basting stitches.

RIGHT AND ABOVE A large array of symbols and patterns decorate this matching sheet and pillow cover, which would look crisp and inviting on any bed.

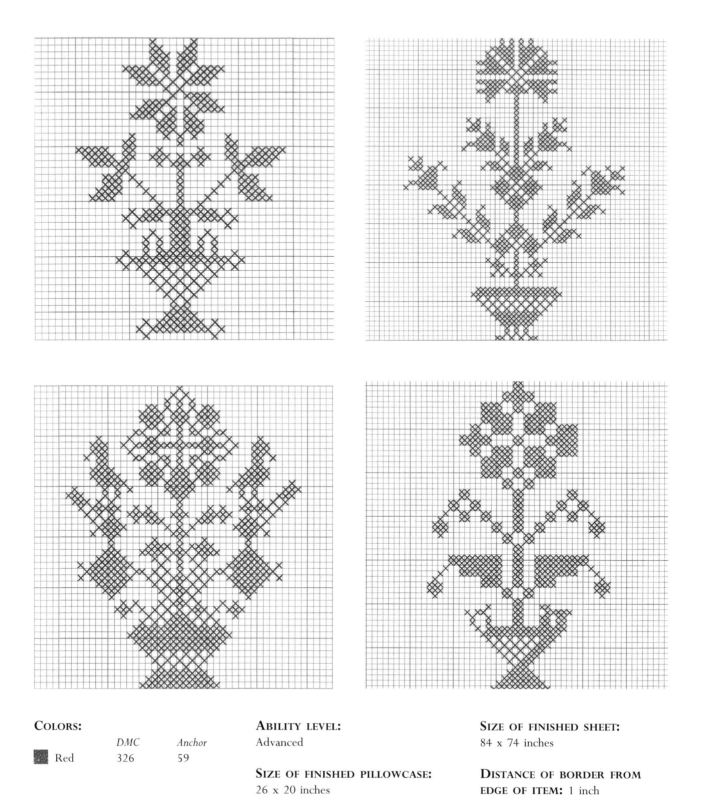

COLORS:

	DMC	Anchor
■ Red	326	59

ABILITY LEVEL:
Advanced

SIZE OF FINISHED PILLOWCASE:
26 x 20 inches

SIZE OF FINISHED SHEET:
84 x 74 inches

DISTANCE OF BORDER FROM EDGE OF ITEM: 1 inch

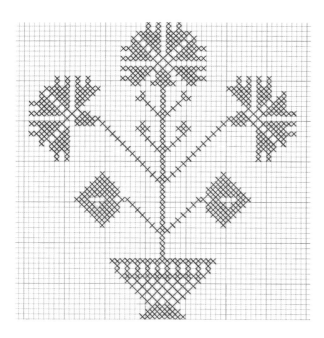

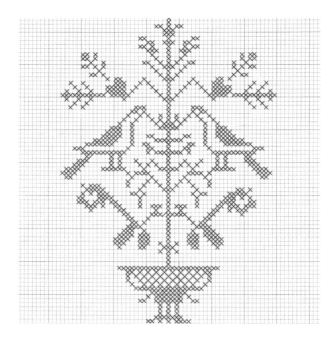

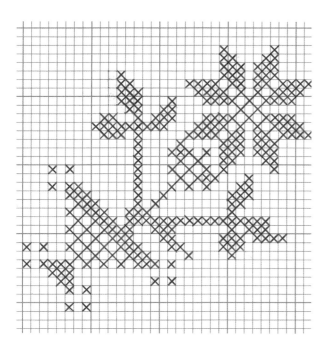

SPACING OF MOTIFS ABOVE BORDER:1¼ inch apart

NUMBER OF STITCHES PER INCH: 16

STRANDED COTTON EMBROIDERY FLOSS: 2 strands

NEEDLE SIZE: 24/26

FABRIC:

White cotton or linen sheeting (at least 76 inches wide)
PILLOWCASE: 1 yard: cut three pieces of fabric: two 34 x 21 inches; the other 7 x 21 inches to form the pocket that holds the pillow in its cover. Cut two pieces for the ruffles at each end, 31 ½ x 9 inches. The cross stitch is worked on one of the large pieces only.
SHEET: 2½ yards: Cut length of sheeting 88 inches long. Use the natural width of the sheet, keeping the selvages rather than sewing hems.

OTHER MATERIALS:

2¼ yards of 3½-inch-wide heavy cotton lace.

TO FINISH

PILLOWCASE

1 First make the ruffles. Fold the strips of fabric in half lengthwise and stitch down each short side, taking a ⅜-inch seam allowance. Trim the

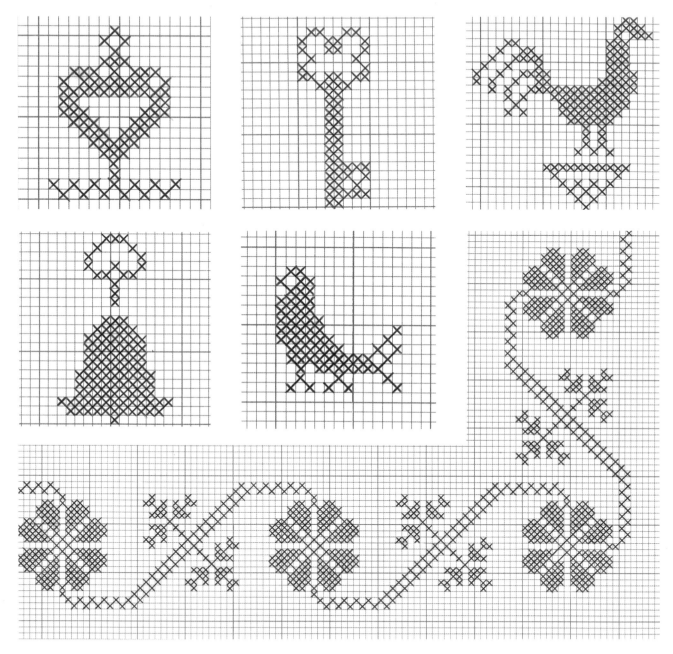

seam back to ¼ inch and clip into the corners. Turn right side out and press. To make the gathered edge, machine stitch with large stitches down the raw edge of each ruffles, ½ inch in from the edge. Pull up the threads, gathering the ruffle until it is

20 inches long. Knot the ends around a pin in order to keep the ruffle the desired length.

2 Take the unembroidered large piece of fabric, and make a hem at one short end by folding over ¼ inch, then

folding over another ⅝ in. Stitch and press. Make another hem on one of the long sides of the fabric that will form the pocket.

3 Lay the cross stitched piece of fabric, right side up, on a flat table.

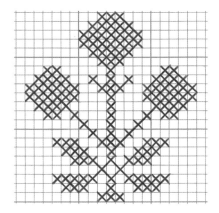

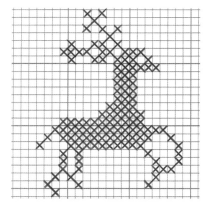

4 Place the other ruffle along the other short edge of the embroidered piece, raw edges together. Place the remaining piece of fabric on it, with the hem up. Line up the raw edges around the other three sides, pin, and machine stitch, taking a ⅜-inch seam. Overlock the raw edges to prevent fraying.

5 Turn the pillowcase right side out and press.

SHEET

1 At the bottom end of the sheet, fold ¼ inch to the wrong side, then a further ⅜ inch. Press, pin, and machine stitch.

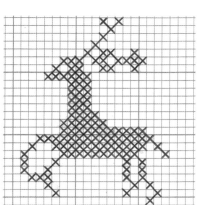

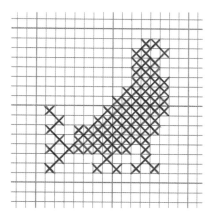

2 At the top of the sheet, fold ¼ inch to the wrong side, then a further 3 inches. Press, pin and machine stitch.

3 If desired, add a border of heavy cotton lace to the top hem.

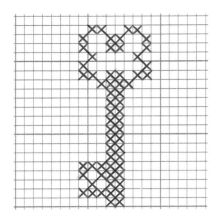

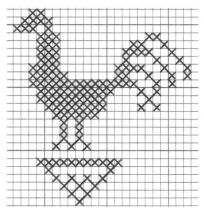

On its right-hand short edge, place one of the ruffles, raw edges together. Place the unhemmed edge of the pocket over the top, matching raw edges. Pin, baste, and machine stitch, taking a ⅜-inch seam allowance. To finish, overlock the

raw edges to prevent fraying. Press. Fold the pocket over so that the seam is hidden and press again. Pin the pocket down so that it stays in place. Turn the whole piece back to the right side.

Feather Bedspread

This unusual bedspread was made in the United States and is one of a matching pair. In fact, it is a plain white hand-sewn quilt which has been embellished with a pattern of cross stitched feathers. When spread out, it looks most effective.

You may not wish to go to the lengths of making your own quilt by hand, but there are various alternatives. Either buy a ready-made quilt, or have one made by a company that specializes in quilting. Do not attempt to make a large quilted item yourself on a sewing machine as it is almost impossible to maneuver the bulk of the fabric around the machine. Otherwise, you could embroider the same design on a simple bedspread. This treatment is not recommended for a duvet, as the constant laundering would eventually damage the cross stitch.

This quilt is the right size for a single bed. However, you could adapt it to a larger bed if desired. The length should be the same, but when plotting the width, add enough extra feathers to cover the top of the bed and to keep the border going around the edge.

LEFT *A four-poster bed is shown off beautifully by fresh blue and white.*
ABOVE *A detail of the cross stitching on the quilted bedspread.*

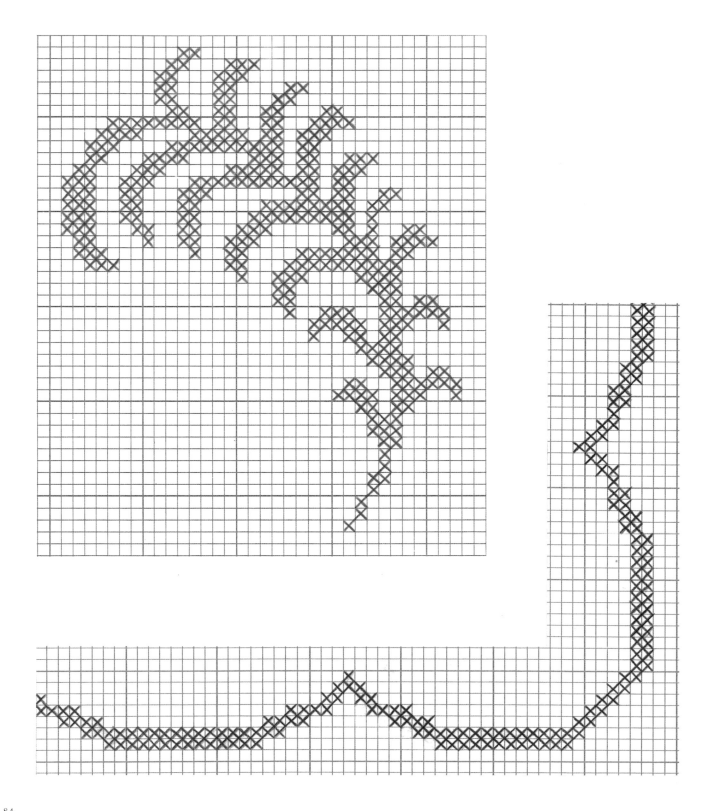

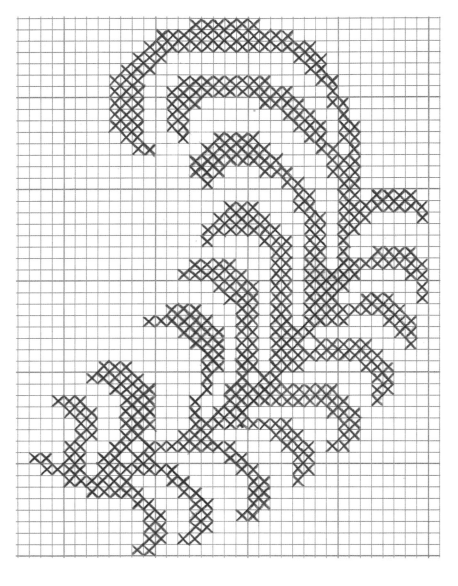

FABRIC:
3 yards white cotton or linen sheeting at least 70 inches wide

TO FINISH
1 Press the cloth so that it is square and even. Carefully trim the edges so that they are straight and square.

2 Either hem the quilt, or bind it with a border of identical fabric.

COLORS:

		DMC	Anchor
▪	Blue	796	133

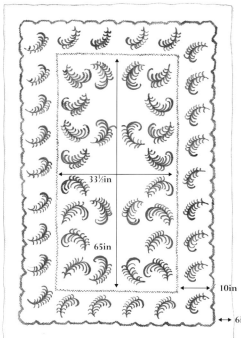

ABILITY LEVEL:
Advanced

SIZE OF FINISHED QUILT:
94 x 65 inches

NUMBER OF STITCHES PER INCH:
6

STRANDED COTTON EMBROIDERY FLOSS: 4 strands

Cradle Cover

This lovely old embroidered coverlet has a Russian feel and portrays a large, handsome peacock in blue and red cotton. Pieces like this were family heirlooms, passed down from generation to generation, as indeed the hand-carved cradle would have been.

This cover is beautifully decorated, not only with the peacock, but also with little patterns and borders which probably had family significances. The peacock is a very ancient motif used in embroidery and appears over and over in antique textiles. It was a sacred and protected bird, often associated with royalty. It symbolized protection, so it is not surprising to see it used on a cradle, to protect the baby from evil.

Why not rekindle the tradition of a family crib cover, and embroider one for the birth of a new family member? This particular one is embroidered on a narrow-loomed linen. It could also be made on wider fabric to be tucked in.

When you are cross stitching with more than one color, it is easier to start with the more dominant color, or with the stronger outline. In this case, again plotting the whole design carefully, it might be best to start with the outline of the peacock's body and move on to its fanned tail feathers.

RIGHT *This delightfully detailed crib cover was probably made in Russia, but is displayed here on a hand-carved Swiss cradle.*

COLORS:

		DMC	Anchor
■	Red	3328	10
■	Blue	930	922

ABILITY LEVEL:
Advanced

SIZE OF FINISHED COVER (EXCLUDING RED LACE AT ENDS):
44 ½ x 15 ¾ inches

NUMBER OF STITCHES PER INCH:
14 small, 7 large

STRANDED COTTON EMBROIDERY FLOSS: 3 strands

NEEDLE SIZE: 24

border of unembroidered cloth all around. First hem the long edges. Fold ¼ inch over to the wrong side, press, then fold over a further ⅜ inch to form a hem. Press.

2 Next, make hems along the two short sides. Fold over ¼ inch to the wrong side, press. Fold over a further ¼ inch, mitering the corners neatly as you go (see page 15). Slipstitch around all four edges. Add matching lace to each end of the coverlet, if desired.

FABRIC:
50 x 18 inches medium-weight cream linen, or Zweigart
28-count fabrics: Pastel Linen 3234 (Color no. 12), or Quaker Cloth 3993 (Linen/cotton, Color no. 222), or Jubilee 3232 (Cotton, Color no. 225)

OTHER MATERIALS:
1 yard of 2-inch-wide heavy cotton lace

TO FINISH
1 Press the embroidered cloth so that it is square and even. Carefully trim away excess fabric, leaving a ⅜ inch

14½in

Accessories

Carnation
Pillow Cover

This charming country-style pillow cover was found in a friend's antique shop in southwest London. It has had considerable wear, but always comes back to life after laundering.

Throw pillows are always useful, and this one is particularly decorative with its bold, simple color. At the time that a lot of items such as these were embroidered, red was the most popular

color, but you might find different colors more sympathetic to your home. The simple motif of flowers is surrounded by a traditional carnation border.

The original cover consists of four identical sections of cross stitch which have been pieced together afterward. Make it in the same way, or stitch all four motifs on one piece of fabric. It has been finished with a border of red and white lace, but if colored lace is hard to find, use a solid color that matches the fabric. The back of the pillow was originally closed with two linen-covered buttons with hand-sewn buttonholes in red cotton. It looks charming and makes for a more old-fashioned look than a modern zipper.

This cover was originally embroidered on a finely woven cotton, but if you find it difficult to stitch on plain fabric, 14-count Aida cloth could be substituted.

LEFT   This cheerful red and white pillow will look at home in any setting.
ABOVE   The square pattern that is repeated in each of the corners.

COLORS:

		DMC	Anchor
■	Red	321	9046

ABILITY LEVEL:
Intermediate

SIZE OF FINISHED COVER:
17 ½ inches square

SIZE OF ONE MOTIF:
 8 x 8 inches

NUMBER OF STITCHES PER INCH:
7

**STRANDED COTTON EMBROIDERY
FLOSS:** 3 strands

NEEDLE SIZE: 20/22

FABRIC FOR CROSS STITCHING:
4 pieces each, 11 inches square
heavyweight linen or cotton, or
20 inches square Zweigart embroidery
fabrics: 14-count Aida 3706 (Cotton,
Color no. 101), or 28-count Quaker
Cloth 3993 (Cotton/Linen, Color no.
101)

OTHER MATERIALS:
Pillow form, approx 17 inches square
2 ¼ yards lace for edging
One piece of similar fabric, to make
the backing, approx 20 inches square

TO FINISH

1 If you have made four separate
panels, join them together evenly,
leaving about ½ inch between the
panels, to make one piece of fabric
approximately 20 inches square.

2 Pin the lace around the four sides
of the fabric, with the sewing line ½
inch out from the cross stitch panels.
Ease it around the corners, adding
some extra fullness. The decorative
edge of the lace should point into the

middle of the pillow cover. Machine
stitch.

3 Place the piece of backing fabric
on top of the cross stitch square,
right sides together. Pin along the
sewing line, around three sides, ½ inch
out from the cross stitch panels.
Machine stitch, taking care to sew
just inside the stitching that is holding
the lace so that the stitching does not
show on the finished cover.

4 Trim the seam on three sides back
to ⅜ inch, and clip the corners
diagonally ⅛ inch from the stitching
line.

5 Turn the cover right side out, and
turn in ⅜ inch on the unfinished side.
Press. Insert the pillow form, and
close the final side with invisible
slipstitches (see page 15).

Rustic Pillow Cover

This rustic pillow was probably made in northern France or Germany. It was acquired from a German textile collector and is appealing for its naive country look. It probably comes from a rural area.

The enlarged snowflake pattern divides into four equal parts and requires careful plotting on the fabric. It has been stitched on a finely woven linen using large stitches, so is quite easy to embroider. An Aida cloth with a corresponding thread count, although easy to use, would look somewhat crude. However, if the unstitched Aida looked ungainly, it would be possible to fill in the background with light-colored cross stitches – definitely good practice for a beginner.

This pillow cover would also look pretty if the edges were piped in brown cording, or had a narrow band of ecru lace around it. The back of the pillow could be made from the same fine linen fabric.

You could then personalize the back by adding your initials, or the date. If it is to be a wedding or birthday present, why not cross stitch the relevant name or names of the recipient, and the date on the back?

RIGHT A country chair with a country pillow. The two look made for each other: rustic, warm, and inviting. The snowflake pattern is reminiscent of northern Europe and may even be Scandinavian in origin.

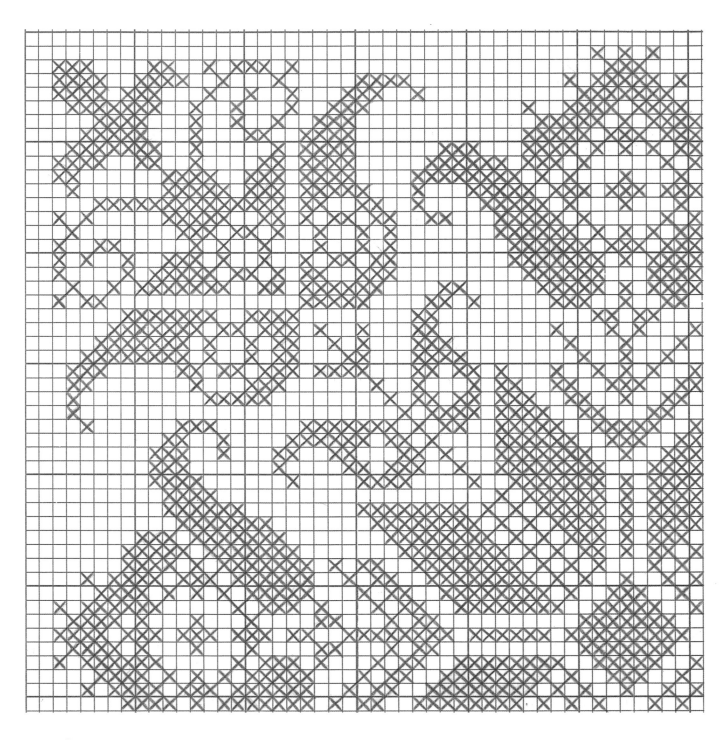

COLORS:

		DMC	Anchor
▓	Brown	400	351

ABILITY LEVEL: Beginner

SIZE OF FINISHED COVER:
20 ½ inch square

SIZE OF WHOLE MOTIF: 15 ¼ inches square

NUMBER OF STITCHES PER INCH:
6

STRANDED COTTON EMBROIDERY FLOSS: 6 strands

NEEDLE SIZE: 22/24

FABRIC FOR CROSS STITCHING:
24-inch of medium-weight ecru, cotton or linen, or
Zweigart 20-count Valerie 3256 (Cotton/Rayon, Color no. 253)

OTHER MATERIALS:
Pillow form, approx 20-inch. One piece of similar fabric for backing, approx 24 inches square

TO FINISH
1 Press the cloth flat and even. Trim the edges of the cloth to leave a border all around 3 inches from the outer edge of the cross stitched design. Trim the other piece of fabric to the same size.

2 Take the plain piece of fabric and place it on top of the cross stitch square, right sides together. Pin around all four side ⅜ inch in from the raw edges.

3 Measure 3 inches down from each corner on one of the sides. The length between these two points will form the hole through which to insert the pillow form. Starting at one of these points, machine stitch up to the corner, around the three sides, and down 3 inches on the fourth side.

4 Trim each corner diagonally, ¼ inch from the stitching. Overlock the raw edges to prevent fraying.

5 Turn the cover right side out, and turn in ⅜ inch on the unfinished side. Press. Insert the pillow form, and close the final side with invisible slipstitches (see page 15).

Tiebacks

Tiebacks, while looking decorative, perform a practical role of holding curtains back from windows to let in the maximum amount of light. They can be made in hundreds of different styles and shapes, but it is rare to find cross stitched tiebacks, so this is a somewhat unique project.

Plain linen curtains hung in the pine windows like this look fresh and simple. The addition of the tiebacks provides a suitable finishing touch, with the crocheted edges in matching mercerized cotton crisp against the cream linen.

Most tiebacks are backed with stiff buckram to give a formal look and shape, and stability against curling or wrinkling. These are lined only in fine cotton, which will work as long as the curtains are lightweight and unlined. Anything heavier will cause the tiebacks to crease and buckle under the weight of the drapery fabric. This could be remedied by adding an interfacing, under the embroidery, of stiff buckram.

The original tiebacks hang in place with metal rings, covered with the same colored thread as used for the cross stitch and the edging. The directions overleaf show how to insert brass rings, but their covering and the edging is not mandatory. However, if you are skilled with a crochet hook, covering the rings will add an authentic finishing touch.

This is a simple but effective project and a good start for an uncomplicated window treatment. Once the tiebacks are completed, you may wish to add a band of matching pattern along the edge of the curtains to complement the tiebacks.

RIGHT Tiebacks add a pretty finishng touch to any window dressing. Here, the simple, sheer curtains are given a charming shape by the tiebacks as well as being made more decorative by the cross stitch detail.

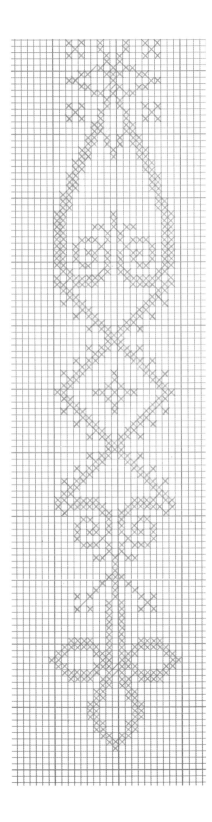

ABILITY LEVEL:
Intermediate

SIZE OF FINISHED TIEBACK:
28 ¼ x 4 inches

NUMBER OF STITCHES PER INCH:
8

**STRANDED COTTON EMBROIDERY
FLOSS:** 4 strands

NEEDLE SIZE: 22/24

**FABRIC FOR CROSS STITCHING —
FOR EACH TIEBACK:**
29 x 4 ½ inches medium-weight
cotton or linen, or
Zweigart 16-count Aida 3251
(Cotton, Color no. 264), or 8-count
Hertarette 3707 (Cotton, Color no.
264), or 32-count Belfast 3609
(Linen, Color no. 222)

**OTHER MATERIALS — FOR EACH
TIEBACK:**
 29 x 4½ inches fine cotton for
backing of tieback
Two 1-inch brass rings

TO FINISH
1 Press the cloth flat and even. Cut a
piece of lining the same size and
shape as the embroidered fabric.

2 Around each side of the tieback,
turn back ⅜ inch to the wrong side.
Pin on the wrong side, close to the
edge. Repeat this process with the
lining, this time making a ½ inch
allowance on each side.

3 With wrong sides together and raw
edges even, put the tieback and lining
together, so that there is a ⅛ inch
gap right around the edge of the
lining. Pin the two together.

4 Insert a brass ring at each end,
between the lining and the tieback,
so that about a ¼ inch protrudes past
the point of the tieback. Hand stitch
in place.

5 Slipstitch the lining to the tieback
(see page 15) around all the edges,
making sure that you cover one side
of the brass rings.

6 If desired, crochet an ornamental
border around the tieback.
Alternatively, bind the edges with
neat blanket stitch (see page 15) or
matching bias binding.

COLORS:

		DMC	Anchor
▨	Gold	383	307

Drapes

In parts of Switzerland, northern Italy, and Austria, mountain farmhouses have small wooden windows adorned with white or cream linen curtains that have been cross stitched by the farmers' wives and daughters. It is still a strong tradition today, and these drapes were found in a Swiss farmhouse.

They were embroidered by the present owner's mother as a gift. They feature several motifs which have been placed in a sort of checkerboard pattern. Most of the motifs consist of blocks of stylized flowers and geometric shapes in red and blue floss. The designs are quite simple to stitch, the skill comes in placing them correctly on the cloth.

Other traditional designs include narrow bands of fabric that are embroidered and then sewn onto the edges of pairs of drapes.

The prettiest part of cross stitched linen curtains is when the light shines through them to show up the patterns, and for this reason they are never lined. In addition, the reverse side needs to be especially neat so no messy loose threads or mistakes can be seen.

The actual curtain sizes have not been given in the following directions (see page 109), so that you can make drapes to fit any of your own windows.

LEFT   Unlined drapes let sunlight in, yet still give a certain amount of privacy. Embroidered drapes, such as these with a checkerboard pattern of motifs, are still a common sight in Switzerland.

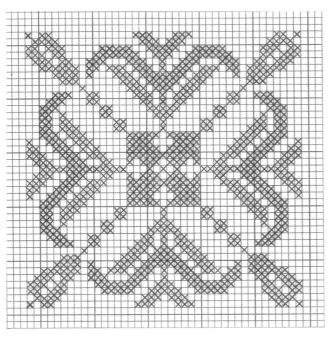

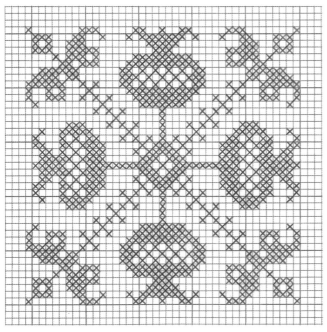
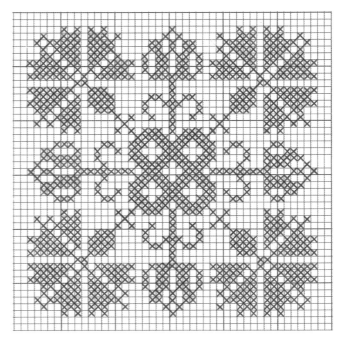

COLORS:

		DMC	Anchor
■	Red	321	9046
■	Blue	796	133

ABILITY LEVEL:
Intermediate

SIZE OF EACH MOTIF:
6 inches square

NUMBER OF STITCHES PER INCH:
7

STRANDED COTTON EMBROIDERY FLOSS: 3 strands

NEEDLE SIZE: 24

FABRIC FOR CROSS STITCHING:
Sheer cotton. Fabric size should equal width of window times 2 to 2 ½ (for gathering); length of window, plus top and bottom hem allowances (see below).

TO FINISH
1 Press the cloth flat and even.

2 Make ½-inch hems down both sides of the drape. Machine stitch, or, to achieve an old-fashioned appearance, hemstitch by hand (see page 15).

3 Make hems at the top and bottom. The depth of the hem will vary, depending on the length of your drapes; short curtains should have hems of at least 2 inches; longer drapes could go to 3 inches. Machine or hemstitch.

4 Attach heading tape along the top edge. Lightweight heading tape designed for glass curtains would be suitable for these curtains.

RIGHT Detail showing the juxtaposition of the various motifs

109

Figured Hand Towel

This treasured hand towel came from France years ago. It is fresh and pleasing, and the quality of linen is superb. Linen makes excellent hand towels due to its excellent absorbent qualities and the fact that it launders superbly, looking crisp and new with very little effort.

Hand towels were popular items for embroidery and made good showpieces for the skills of the needlewomen. This finely worked piece is the work of a very accomplished embroiderer. Its lace-like border is formed of complex, pulled-thread work and needle weaving made from the same, single piece of fabric that supports the cross stitch. It was no doubt the work of the original embroiderer. I am not sure I would give over such fine and skilled workmanship to the drying of hands!

The measurements below are given from the plain top of the towel to the bottom edge of the narrow embroidered strip. You could make a hand towel to these measurements with just a plain strip of cloth between the two parts of the cross stitch, or you could reproduce the original more exactly by inserting 2-inch-wide cotton lace between the two parts of the towel and another piece along the bottom.

RIGHT This fine towel looks impressive with its lacy border of expert drawn-thread work, made from the main embroidery fabric. Considering the amount of wear it would have received, it is surprising that it has survived in such good condition.

Dotted lines indicate center of design

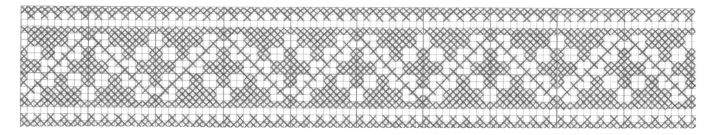

ABILITY LEVEL:
Intermediate

SIZE OF FINISHED TOWEL:
(from top of towel to bottom of strip):32 ¼ x 15 inches

SIZE OF EMBROIDERED PANEL:
15 x 4 ½ inches

SIZE OF EMBROIDERED STRIP:
15 x 1 ⅜ inches

NUMBER OF STITCHES PER INCH
13

STRANDED COTTON EMBROIDERY FLOSS: 3 strands

NEEDLE SIZE: 24

FABRIC:
34 x 20 inch lightweight white linen or cotton, or
Zweigart 25-count Dublin 3604 (Linen, Color no. 100); 27-count Linda 1235 (Cotton, Color no. 1)

TO FINISH
1 Press the cloth so that it is square and even. Carefully trim away excess fabric, leaving a ⅝-inch border of unembroidered cloth around the long edges and one short edge of the design. Check the overall length of the piece, and adjust if necessary.

2 Fold ¼ inch over to the wrong side around the three cut edges.

3 Press. Then fold a further ⅜ inch over to form a hem. Miter the corners (see page 15) and pin. Slipstitch in place (see page 15).

COLORS:

	DMC	Anchor
▦ Red	321	9046

BELOW Detail showing the fine cross stitching of the panel.

Book Covers

Precious books often have cloth covers for protecting leather and gilded bindings. In some churches, all the prayer books and hymn books have embroidered covers, sewn with loving care by church members.

The book covers shown here are German, and are probably

the work of children. For many years in Europe, part of every girl's education was to learn embroidery, starting with cross stitch on book covers, samplers, and the like. Border patterns were mainly chosen to practice good needlework, and the work often displayed the initials of the embroiderer and the year. The strong colors on both covers are typical of Germany and central Europe, but the designs would also look effective in softer, pastel colors.

A prayer book with a cross stitched, personalized cover would make a lovely baptism or confirmation present for a child. A photograph or special family album could be similarly covered, but be careful to use a tightly woven linen for bigger books, so the cover doesn't sag in the middle. You could also make up your own pattern by drawing it on graph paper first, then carefully plotting it on to the cloth. When covering very thick books, do remember to allow enough fabric to reach around the spine of the book.

LEFT Precious antique books can be preserved with ornamental cloth book covers.
ABOVE A typical design shows the owner's initials and the date.

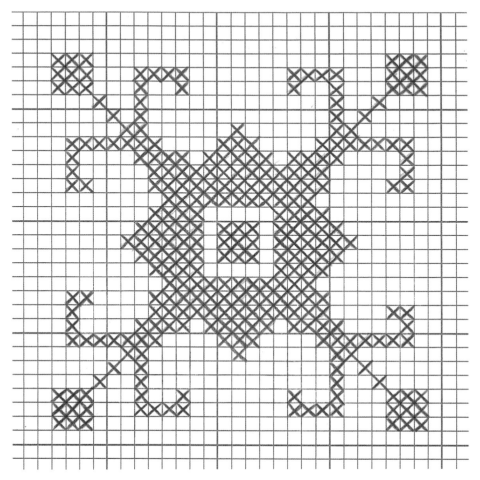

ABILITY LEVEL:
Beginner

SIZE OF FINISHED COVERS (OPEN):
Red and Blue: 7 ½ x 15 ¾ inches

Red and Black: 9 ½ x 15 inches

NUMBER OF STITCHES PER INCH:
10

STRANDED COTTON EMBROIDERY FLOSS: 4 strands

NEEDLE SIZE: 24

FABRIC:
28 x 12 inches open-weave cotton or linen, or Zweigart 20-count Valerie 3256 (Cotton/Rayon, Color no. 264)

TO FINISH
1 Press the cloth so that it is square and even. Carefully trim away excess fabric so that there is 1 inch outside the cross stitch design on each long side, and enough for a turnback of 6 inches along each short side.

2 Make a hem on each short side by turning ⅛ inch over to the wrong side, and then turning over a further ⅜ inch. Pin, machine or slipstitch (see page 15), and press.

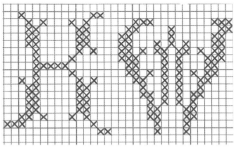

COLORS:

		DMC	Anchor
■	Red	321	9046
■	Blue	311	133
▦	Black	310	403

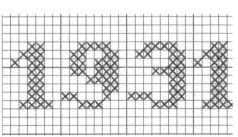

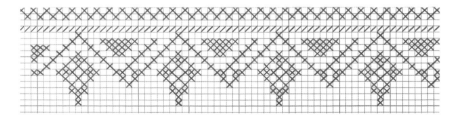

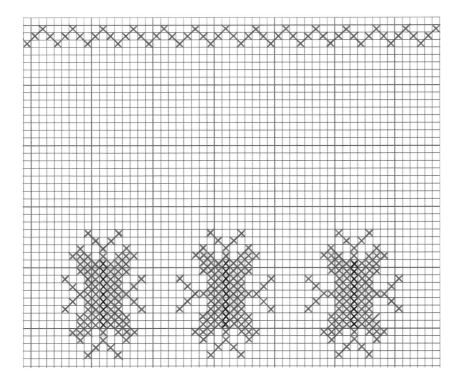

3 To prevent fraying, overlock the raw edges along each long side, using a fine zigzag or buttonhole stitch.

4 With right sides together, fold each short side back on itself by 5 inches. (This is to form the pockets that will hold the cover of the book.) Pin at the edges, and machine stitch (or backstitch), taking a ⅝ inch seam allowance. Cut into the corners, and turn right side out.

5 Fold the seam over neatly in between the pockets, where the spine of the book will go. Stitch the edge of the seam down at this place with a few neat hand stitches.

6 RED AND BLUE COVER: To make the ties, cut six 24-inch-long pieces of embroidery thread: cut four in red and two in blue. Put them all together and fold them in half. Pin the loop at the end of the fold to something stable, and braid the threads together as far as possible. Knot the ends neatly and trim.

7 Sew the knotted ends to the edge of the book cover. Make two blue tassels (see page 69), and attach them to the loop ends of the ties.

Lavender Sachets

Lavender has been grown for centuries, not only for its delicate fragrance, but also for its healing qualities. It is known that the ancient Egyptians used it to scent their clothes and rooms, and in later centuries, bags containing dried lavender flowers were put in drawers and wardrobes to perfume household linens. In addition to being pleasant to smell, lavender has been found to ward off the clothes moth that can cause so much damage to wool fabrics.

Cross stitching lends itself beautifully to decorating little bags, and can take the form of initials or simple motifs. Although some suggestions follow here, any letters or designs in other parts of this book could be adapted for this purpose. Stitch the embroidery on an outer bag, then make little cotton liners to hold the lavender, so that it can be replaced without disturbing the back of the embroidery. Make sure you buy good quality lavender as the scent lingers much longer.

These bags are very easy to make and are quite suitable for beginners. They are joined with a seam down the center back, so the initial must be embroidered exactly in the middle of the piece of fabric. Then, when the bag is sewn up, the initial will appear in the correct place on the front side.

RIGHT An inviting array of little embroidered lavender sachets. They make an ideal project for cross stitch beginners, especially when made from an open-weave fabric.

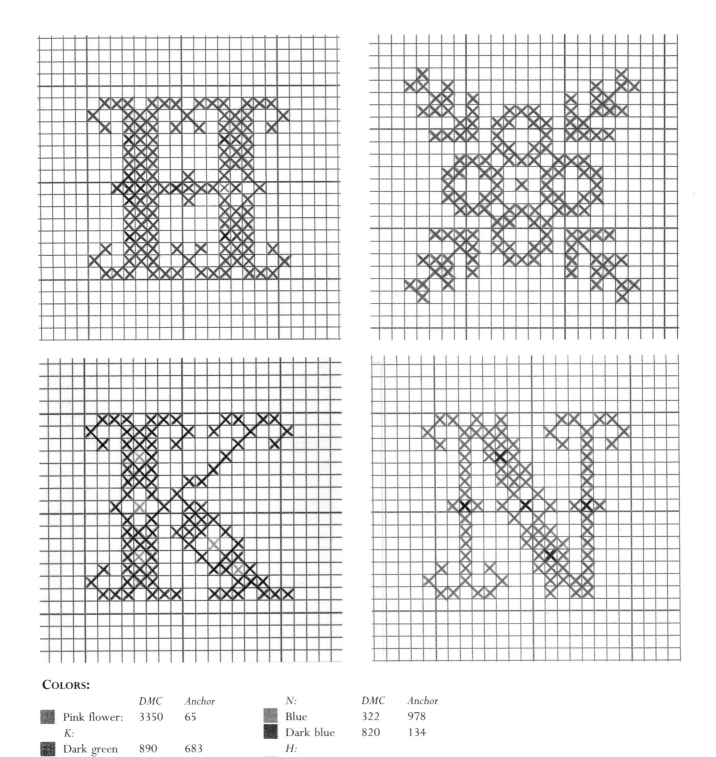

COLORS:

		DMC	Anchor
■	Pink flower:	3350	65
	K:		
■	Dark green	890	683
■	Yellow	445	288
■	Light green	3348	264

		DMC	Anchor
	N:		
■	Blue	322	978
■	Dark blue	820	134
	H:		
■	Red	321	9046
■	Wine	902	72

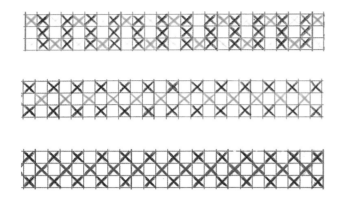

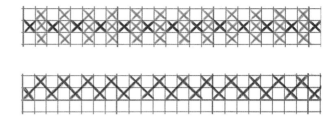

ABILITY LEVEL:
Beginner

SIZE OF FINISHED BAG:
3 ½ x 2 ¼ inches

NUMBER OF STITCHES PER INCH:
14

STRANDED COTTON EMBROIDERY FLOSS: 2 strands

NEEDLE SIZE: 24/26

FABRIC:
4 x 5 inches cotton or linen, or Zweigart 14-count Aida 3706 (Cotton, Color no. 101); 28-count Jubilee 3232 (Cotton, Color no. 1)

OTHER MATERIALS:
For each bag: ribbon ¼ -inch in width

TO FINISH
1 Press the cloth so that it is square and even.

2 Fold the fabric in half, with right sides together, and matching all the raw edges. Firs pin along the center back, with a ¼ -inch seam. Then hand or machine stitch. With the seam in the center back, press the seam open.

3 Stitch across the bottom of the bag with a ¼-inch seam.

4 Turn the bag right side out. Turn over ¼ inch to the inside and press flat.

5 Fill the bag with lavender and stitch ¾ inch along the edge.

6 Insert a 2-inch ribbon loop with 1 ½ inch visible above the top, and stitch it into the seam as you stitch the rest bag closed along the rest of the seam.

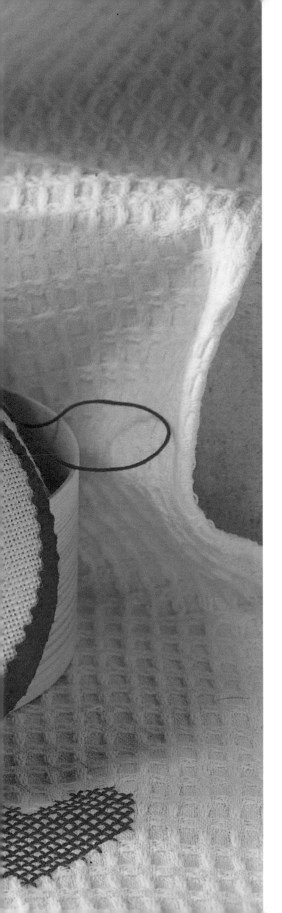

Pincushion Boxes

As long as textiles have been woven, they have also needed with use, repairing and darning. So there has always been a need for storing sewing implements. These vary from the modern, large, purpose-made compartmentalized boxes to old-fashioned drawstring sacks with ivory and bone handles. With the development of mass-produced steel pins and needles came a need for the pincushion. Over the centuries, it has taken many forms, from little folding suede purses to heavily embroidered, decorative cushions. The Victorians even used beadwork to ornament pincushions.

These little boxes with their padded lids make wonderful presents. Their uses need not be restricted to sewing implements: I use mine for jewelry and precious odds and ends.

The embroidery is simple, and the flat fabric can then be glued to the lids of little wooden boxes. Decorative matching braid glued around the edge hides frayed ends and glue marks.

Sizes are not given below as they will depend on the sort of boxes available. However, when choosing a box, bear in mind the size of the finished motifs to make sure they will fit on the box's lid. If you wish to make them larger or smaller, just use a fabric with a larger or smaller thread count.

LEFT AND ABOVE Typical of the eastern part of Switzerland, these little boxes make a lovely present, especially when personalized with an initial.

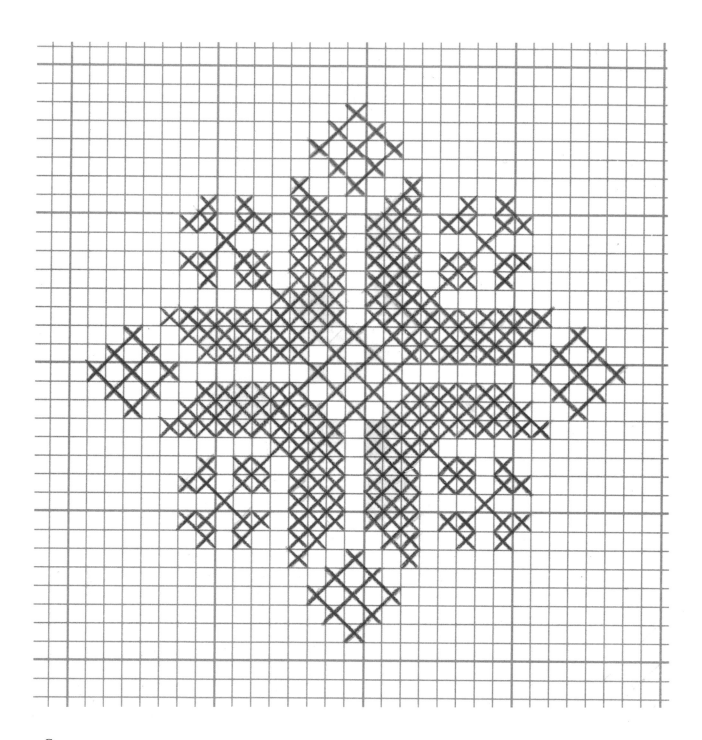

COLORS:

		DMC	Anchor
▨	Red	321	9046
▨	Blue	796	133

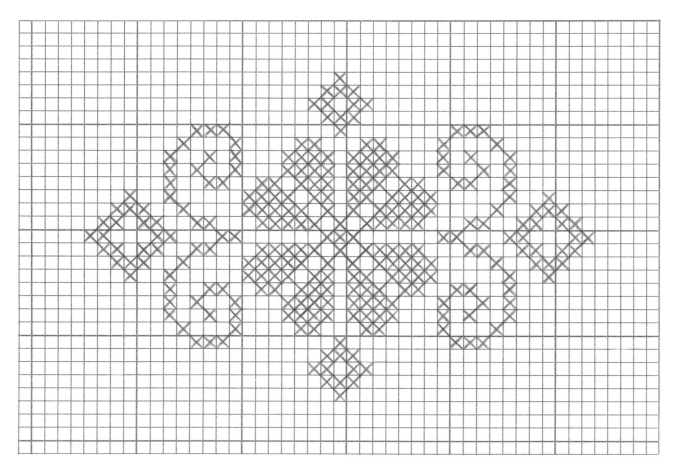

ABILITY LEVEL:
Beginner

SIZE OF MOTIFS: Red 2 ¼ x 2 ¼
inches; Blue 3 ¼ x 2 inches

NUMBER OF STITCHES PER INCH:
12

**STRANDED COTTON EMBROIDERY
FLOSS:** 2 strands

NEEDLE SIZE: 24/26

FABRIC:
Amount depends on size of box.
Allow enough for padding on lid and
to reach down sides of lid.
Use medium-weight white cotton or
linen, or Zweigart 25-count Lugana
3835 (Cotton/Rayon, Color no. 100)

TO FINISH

1 Press the cloth so that it is straight
and even.

2 Pad the lid of the box with batting,
or soft absorbent cotton. Apply all
purpose glue to the sides of the box,
and then stretch the embroidered
fabric in place, down over the sides,
taking tucks in it to fit the lid, as
necessary. While the glue is drying,
hold the fabric in place with a large
rubber band.

3 Trim the fabric around the edges of
the lid. Cut enough braid to go
around the lid, and glue on, covering
all the tucks and edges. Hold in place
with a rubber band while drying, if
necessary.

Index

accessories 92-125
  book covers 114-17
  curtains 106-9
  drapes 106-9
  hand towels 110-13
  lavender bags 118-21
  pillow covers 95-7,
    98-101
  pincushions 122-5
  tiebacks 102-5
advanced projects
  cradle cover 86-91
  feather bedspread 82-5
  house sampler 32-7
  red and blue tablecloth
    62-5
  reindeer runner 70-3
  sheets and pillowcases
    76-81
  zigzag cloth 66-9
Aida cloth 12
alphabet sampler 18-23
animals 70-3, 81
Austria 59, 62, 107

bed drapes 11
bed linen 74-92
  cot cover 86-91
  feather bedspread 82-5
  sheets and pillowcases
    76-81
Bedouins 8-9
bedspreads 8, 82-5
beginners' projects
  book covers 114-17
  lavender sachets 118-21
  napkins/napkin rings 41-3
  pillow covers 98-101
  pincushions 122-5
  table mats 44-9
birds 80-1
  heraldic 32

peacocks 58-61, 86-91
blanket stitch 15
book covers 114-17
borders
  placemats 46-7
  pulled thread 110
  with tassels 67, 69
  tiebacks 105
  working method 25
Bostake, Jane 11
brown pillow cover 98-101
buckram 43, 102
Burma 8

candlestick mat 48
carnations
  pillow cover 95
  sheets 76
  symbolism 55, 76
  tablecloth 54-7
China 8
cleanliness 12
cloth see fabric
clothing 9, 11
colorfast thread 14, 55, 67
corners, mitered 15
cotton, stranded 14
count, fabric 12
cradle cover 86-91
cross stitch
  Danish 50
  European 9, 10-11
  flattened 50
  history 8-11
  long armed 9
  starting 14
  technique 14
curtains 106-9
  tie-backs 102-5

Danish cross stitch 50

designs, plotting 14-15, 18,
    27, 70, 76, 115
dowry hangings 8
drawn-thread work 15, 59,
    110

Eastern Europe 66-9
edging 44, 57, 59, 76, 98
England 25-31, 32-7, 95
European cross stitch 9, 10-11

fabric
  book covers 115
  count 12
  gingham 44
  types to use 12-14
feather bedspread 82-5
finishing techniques 15
flattened cross stitch 50
floss, stranded 14
flowers 79-81
  carnations 54, 76, 95
  roses 50-3
  stylized 9, 32, 95, 107-9
framing 32
France 98, 110
fringes
  knotted 62, 65
  see also tassels

geometric patterns 8, 107-9
Germany 18, 59, 62, 98, 115
gingham mat 44, 49
Grace Shaw sampler 24-9
Greece 9

hand towel 110-13
hemstitch 15, 59, 110
herringbone stitch 15

Herta cloth 12
house sampler 30-5

interfacing 102
intermediate projects
    carnation tablecloth 54-7
    curtain tiebacks 102-5
    drapes 107-9
    cushion covers 95-7
    hand towel 110-13
    peacock tablecloth 58-61
    pillow covers 95-7
    rose tablecloth 50-3
    samplers 17-38
ironing 15, 30
Italy 9, 107

knots
    fringe 62, 65
    thread 14

Laos 8
laundering 14, 41, 55, 76, 83
lavender sachets 118-21
light
    protection from 18
    when working 12
linen
    curtains 102
    samplers 13, 17
    tablecloth with panels 62
    uses 11, 12
    see also bed linen;
        table linen

material see fabric
mats, table 44-9
Mexico 8
mitered corners 15

Morocco 8, 9
motifs, positioning 15
napkins 41-2, 70
    napkin rings 41, 43
needles 14

panels, in tablecloths 62-5
peacocks
    cradle cover 86-91
    symbolism 59, 86
    tablecloth 58-61
peasants 8, 10
pillowcases 76-81
pillow covers
    brown 98-101
    red and white 95-7
pincushions 122-5
place mats 41, 44-9
    four-heart border 46
    with narrow border 47
Portugal 9
projects
    accessories 92-125
    bed linen 74-92
    samplers 16-35
    table linen 39-73
    see also advanced
        beginners'
        intermediate
pulled-thread work 15, 59,
    110

quilts, feather bedspread 82-5

red and blue tablecloth 62-5
red thread 9, 11, 55
    symbolism 11
red and white pillow cover
    95-7
reindeer runner 70-3

religion 9, 25, 114-17
rituals 9
rose tablecloth 50-3
runner, reindeer 70-3
Russia 8
Shaker style 11
samplers 17-37
    alphabet 18-23
    Grace Shaw 23-29
    historical 11
    house 30-5
scissors 12
Shaw, Grace 23-9
sheets 76-81
silks 14
slipstitch 15
snowflake pattern 98-101
South America 8
Spain 9
stitches
    blanket stitch 15
    cross stitch 14
    hemstitch 15
    herringbone 15
    slipstitch 15
stranded floss 14
styles 8, 11
Switzerland 44-9, 62-5,
    70-3, 107
symbolism
    carnations 55, 76
    peacocks 59, 86
    red 11

table linen 38-73
    napkins/napkin rings 41-3
    runner 70-3
    table mats 44-9
    tablecloths 50-69
table mats 41, 44-9
    for candlestick 48
    gingham 49

tablecloths 50-69
    carnation 54-7
    peacock 58-61
    red and blue 62-5
    rose 50-3
    zigzag cloth 66-9
tapestry needles 14
tassels
    border 67, 69
    fringe 62, 65
technique 11, 14
Thailand 8
thread
    colorfast 14, 55, 67
    red 9, 11, 55
    samplers 11
    starting work 14
    types 11, 14
tiebacks 102-5
towels, hand 110-13

United States 11, 82-5
Uzbekistan 8

wall hangings 11
weave, fabric 12
weddings 9, 11, 55, 76, 98

zigzag cloth 66-9

Acknowledgments

Many thanks to Ernst Hämmerle, curator of the Heimatmuseum in Davos, Switzerland, for allowing us to photograph there, and for all his help and enthusiasm. Also to Guolf Gattiker and his family in Bergün, Switzerland, for their kind hospitality.

Thank you, Anna and Johnnie Werth in Davos, for all your help during photography.

Most of the pieces in this book are from my own collection, but some came from fellow collectors, and my thanks go to them: Marian Goder, Angel Hughes from Tobias and the Angel, Fiona King from Charleville Gallery, all at Shaker, Val Crowther from Antiques and Things, all at Lacquer Chest, Violette Gurr from Harwood Antiques, Annie Stevens, and Marlis Stoop.

Thanks to Margot Richardson, a terrific and calm editor! And finally, to my wonderful Swiss mother, who taught me how to cross stitch.